MAKING SENSE OF **HISTORY**
1745–1901

JOHN D. CLARE

NEIL BATES

ALEC FISHER

RICHARD KENNETT

ECLIPSE

DYNAMIC LEARNING

HODDER EDUCATION
AN HACHETTE UK COMPANY

The Schools History Project

Set up in 1972 to bring new life to history for students aged 13–16, the Schools History Project continues to play an innovatory role in secondary history education. From the start, SHP aimed to show how good history has an important contribution to make to the education of a young person. It does this by creating courses and materials which both respect the importance of up-to-date, well-researched history and provide enjoyable learning experiences for students.

Since 1978 the Project has been based at Trinity and All Saints University College Leeds. It continues to support, inspire and challenge teachers through the annual conference, regional courses and website: http://www.schoolshistoryproject.org.uk. The Project is also closely involved with government bodies and awarding bodies in the planning of courses for Key Stage 3, GCSE and A level.

The Publishers would like to thank the following for permission to reproduce copyright material:

Photo credits
p.2 © INTERFOTO / Alamy; **p.3** © Hulton Archive/Getty Images; **p.5** © Realimage / Alamy; **p.6** © Illustrated London News Ltd/Mary Evans Picture Library ; **p.8** © Hulton-Deutsch Collection/Corbis ; **p.10** © World History Archive / TopFoto ; **p.11** tr © TopFoto, cl © Mary Evans Picture Library, br © Gretchen Gauthier ; **p.12** t © World History Archive, / TopFoto, b © Science and Society/SuperStock ; **p.13** t © 2001 Topham Picturepoint/TopFoto, cl © stupot7777 – Fotolia, cr © The Granger Collection, NYC / TopFoto, b The 'Frog' Plate, 1774 (ceramic), Wedgwood, Josiah (1730-95) / © Salisbury Museum / Bridgeman Images ; **p.14** tr © Christie's Images Ltd/SuperStock, bl © DeAgostini/Getty Images) ; **p.15** © Mary Evans Picture Library ; **p.16** © Print Collector / HIP / TopFoto ; **p.17** © The Art Archive/Alamy ; **p.18** t © 2003 Topham Picturepoint/TopFoto, b © Lordprice Collection / Alamy ; **p.19** tl © Travel21 Impact / Heritage Images / TopFoto, tr © The Granger Collection, NYC / TopFoto ; **p.22** © World History Archive / Alamy ; **p.24** © Heritage Image Partnership Ltd / Alamy ; **p.26** © The Art Archive / Alamy ; **p.28** © Snap Stills/REX ; **p.30** The Rabbits, 1792 (copper engraving) (colour photo), English School, (18th century) / © Private Collection / Bridgeman Images ; **p.34** © The Granger Collection, NYC / TopFoto ; **p.35** © nickolae – Fotolia; **p.36** t © Amoret Tanner / Alamy, b © Mary Evans Picture Library ; **p.37** © Lordprice Collection / Alamy ; **p.38** Duria antiquior (Ancient Dorset), an imaginative reconstruction of the life of the Jurassic seas, engraved by George Scharf (1820-95) printed by Charles Joseph Hullmandel (1789-1850) (engraving), De La Beche, Henry Thomas (1796-1855) (after) / © Oxford University Museum of Natural History, UK / Bridgeman Images ; **p.39** © World History Archive / Alamy ; **p.41** © Lebrecht Music and Arts Photo Library / Alamy ; **p.43** © The Granger Collection, NYC / TopFoto ; **p.44** The Reformers' Attack on the Old Rotten Tree, or the Foul Nests of the Cormorants in Danger, satirical cartoon, pub. by E. King, c.1831 / British Library, London, UK / © British Library Board. All Rights Reserved / Bridgeman Images ; **p.45** © Universal History Archive/Getty Images ; **p.47** t © Mary Evans Picture Library / Alamy, b © Punch Limited ; **p.49** © interfoto/SuperStock ; **p.50** © Guildhall Library & Art Gallery/Heritage Images/Getty Images ; **p.51** © TopFoto ; **p.52** t Courtesy of The Lewis Walpole Library, Yale University, b © Hartlepool Borough Council ; **p.53** © NDP / Alamy ; **p.54** © Punch Limited ; **p.55** © World History Archive / Alamy ; **p.56, p.57** © c – Fotolia ; **p.58** © Punch Limited ; **p.60** © Neil Bates; **p.62** © National Folklore Collection, University College Dublin ; **p.63** l © Imagestate Media Partners Limited - Impact Photos / Alamy r Courtesy Liam Kennedy ; **p.64** © Universal Images Group/SuperStock ; **p.65** t © Neil Bates, b © Bridgeman Images / TopFoto ; **p.66** © Andrew McConnell / Alamy ; **p.68** t © Radharc Images / Alamy, b © John Cole / Alamy ; **p.72, p.73** © The Granger Collection, NYC / TopFoto ; **p.73** r © The Granger Collection, NYC / TopFoto ; **p.74** Natives of New South Wales as seen in the streets of Sydney, plate 4 of part 1 of 'Views in New South Wales and Van Diemen's Land', printed by C. Hullmandel, (litho), Earle, Augustus (1793-1838) (after) / © National Library of Australia, Canberra, Australia / Bridgeman Images ; **p.75** Cartoon by Udo J.Keppler; Library of Congress Prints and Photographs Division ; **p.76** © Stock Montage, Inc. / Alamy ; **p.77** © kmiragaya – Fotolia ; **p.84** A Tour through the British Colonies and Foreign Possessions (colour litho), English School, (19th century) / © Private Collection / The Stapleton Collection / Bridgeman Images ; **p.85** © TopFoto ; **p.86** © FALKENSTEINFOTO / Alamy ; **p.87** India: The Rani of Jhansi (1835-1858) in a 19th century Kalighat painting / Pictures From History / © Bridgeman Images ; **p.88** © Mary Evans Picture Library ; **p.89** © Geraint Lewis / Alamy ; **p.92** Revolutionary cartoon about 'Tithes, Taxes and Graft' (coloured engraving), French School, (18th century) / © Musee de la Ville de Paris, Musee Carnavalet, Paris, France / Bridgeman Images ; **p.93** © DeAgostini/Getty Images ; **p.96** © Roger-Viollet / TopFoto ; **p.97** t © TopFoto, b © Roger-Viollet / TopFoto ; **p.98** © 2005 Roger-Viollet / Topfoto ; **p.99** © World History Archive / TopFoto ; **p.100** t © Richard Kennett, b © The Gallery Collection/Corbis ; **p.101** © World History Archive / TopFoto ; **p.104** tl © Universal Images Group/SuperStock, cr © Fine Art Images / Heritage Images / TopFoto, bl © Christie's Images/Corbis ; **p.105** t Quatre-Bras 1815, 1875 (oil on canvas), Butler, Lady (Elizabeth Southerden Thompson) (1846-1933) / © National Gallery of Victoria, Melbourne, Australia / Bridgeman Images, b

© British Library Board / TopFoto ; **p.108** © Ilya S. Saucnok / Getty Images ; **p.110** t © Mary Evans Picture Library b © matd – Fotolia ; **p112**, **p.113** Haymaking in Hampshire, Meadows, James Edwin (1828-88) / Private Collection / Photo © Bonhams, London, UK / Bridgeman Images ; **p.114**, **p.115** © Everett Collection Historical / Alamy ; **p.116**, **p.117** © The Keasbury-Gordon Photograph Archive / Alamy ; **p.119** t © Mary Evans Picture Library b © match – Fotolia ; **p.122** l Returned from Market, engraved by W. Annis, pub. by Morgan & Pearce, 1803 (mezzotint engraving), Wheatley, Francis (1747-1801) (after) / © Private Collection / Bridgeman Images, r © Mary Evans Picture Library ; **p.124** t © liszt collection / Alamy, bl © Amoret Ianner / Alamy, br © TopFoto ; p.126 © Neil Bates ; **p.127** © TopFoto ; **p.128** l © Pixtal/Superstock, c © Ralph Hutchings/Visuals Unlimited, Inc./Science Photo Library, r © Biophoto Associates/Science Photo Library ; **p.130** r © Peter Higginbotham Collection / Mary Evans Picture Library, l © British Library Board / Topfoto ; **p.133** © Barnardo's / TopFoto ; **p.135** © British Library Board / TopFoto.

Text acknowledgements

Every effort has been made to trace all copyright holders, but if any have been inadvertently overlooked the Publishers will be pleased to make the necessary arrangements at the first opportunity.

Answers to activity 2 on page 109: Marxist = A, F, Revisionist = C, D, Post-Revisionist = B, E.

Although every effort has been made to ensure that website addresses are correct at time of going to press, Hodder Education cannot be held responsible for the content of any website mentioned in this book. It is sometimes possible to find a relocated web page by typing in the address of the home page for a website in the URL window of your browser.

Hachette UK's policy is to use papers that are natural, renewable and recyclable products and made from wood grown in sustainable forests. The logging and manufacturing processes are expected to conform to the environmental regulations of the country of origin.

Orders: please contact Bookpoint Ltd, 130 Milton Park, Abingdon, Oxon OX14 4SB. Telephone: +44 (0)1235 827720. Fax: +44 (0)1235 400454. Lines are open 9.00a.m.–5.00p.m., Monday to Saturday, with a 24-hour message answering service. Visit our website at www.hoddereducation.co.uk

© John D. Clare, Neil Bates, Alec Fisher, Richard Kennett

First published in 2015 by

Hodder Education,

An Hachette UK company

338 Euston Road

London NW1 3BH

Impression number 10 9 8 7 6 5 4 3 2 1

Year 2019 2018 2017 2016 2015

Cover photo © Science and Society / SuperStock

Illustrations by Barking Dog Art, Peter Lubach, Tony Randell and Sebastian Quigley

Design layouts by Lorraine Inglis Design

Typeset in PMN Caecilia Light 10/13pt

Printed in Italy

A catalogue record for this title is available from the British Library

ISBN 978 14718 05981

Contents

Investigating 1745–1901

The Great Exhibition of 1851

This series starts each textbook by studying an event which the author team thinks defines the age – the event which says most about what the period was like and best gives us a sense of the period. For this book, we have chosen the Great Exhibition in 1851; pages 2–3 will give you a chance to consider what it tells us about the times.

On 1 May 1851 Queen Victoria opened the Great Exhibition in London. It was housed in the Crystal Palace – a specially built, iron-framed building with 293,655 panes of glass, covering 7.6 hectares. Among the 100,000 exhibits from all over the world was the fabulous Koh-I-Noor diamond, recently acquired from India. Sunday opening was not allowed, and there was no smoking, no dogs and no alcohol. Schweppes paid £5,500 for the contract to provide refreshments, and sold 1,092,337 bottles of soft drinks.

The Exhibition certainly created a stir at the time. Six million visitors went to see it. *The Times* called it 'a fairy palace within walls of glass and iron' and a German visitor declared it: 'a spectacle such as the world will scarcely behold again'.

B

⬆ This **lithograph** shows part of the India display.

A

A description of the Great Exhibition

On entering the building for the first time, the eye is completely dazzled ... We have here the Indian Court, Africa, Canada, the West Indies ... Sheffield and its hardware, the woollen and mixed cloth, printing and dyeing ... general hardware, brass and iron-work of all kinds, locks, grates ... agricultural machines and implements ... the mineral products of England ... cotton and woollen power-looms in motion ... rope-making lathes, marine engines, hydraulic presses, steam machinery ... Persia, Greece, Egypt, and Turkey, France, its tapestry, machinery, arms and instruments, occupying two large courts ... and the United States, with its agricultural implements, raw materials etc. ...

In the British half are the silks and shawls, lace and embroideries, jewellery and clocks and watches, behind them military arms and models, chemicals, naval architecture, philosophical instruments, civil engineering, musical instruments, anatomical models, glass chandeliers ... on the opposite side perfumery, toys, fishing materials, wax flowers and stained glass.

The Art Journal (1851).

C

⬆ This lithograph from the time shows the exhibits in the main nave (which was 563 metres long and 124 metres wide). Note the use of a word usually used in reference to a church to describe the building.

Activity

1 Working in a group of two or three, study the information on pages 2–3 and find one fact which seems to reveal something about each of the following:

▮ society (such as power and wealth, leisure and entertainment, fashion, the place of women, the lives of ordinary people)

▮ the economy (such as industry and technology, buildings)

▮ beliefs and attitudes (such as religion, morality, empire).

For each, explain what it reveals about the people of the time.

2 Discuss as a class: 'What does the Great Exhibition tell us about the period 1745–1901?'

3 Suggest reasons why the Great Exhibition was held. Support your suggestions with facts and explanation.

Welcome to the Age of ...?

Earlier in your course you have studied a period which everybody since the Renaissance has called 'the Middle Ages', and a period covering the years 1509–1745 which many people term 'the Early Modern Era'. The twentieth century is easily termed 'the Modern Age'. But there is no generally accepted name for the years 1745–1901.

The years 1745–1901 were a time of explosive change in every area of life. The population of Great Britain grew from 7 million to 37 million. There were massive changes in the economy and technology. Britain gained a worldwide empire. There were violent changes in politics – though less so in England than elsewhere – and in people's beliefs.

Perhaps this is why historians have been unable to find just one term which sums up the era. One historian has called it 'the Age of Transformation', another 'the Age of Revolutions', but many other words have been used, depending on what different historians have judged the key aspects of the period.

Historians who see it mainly as a time of economic growth often call it 'the Age of Industry'. Historians who are positive about the changes which occurred tend to use names such as Progress, Reform and even Elegance. Historians who have studied the negative underbelly of the period have called it 'the Gilded Age' and 'the Age of Faking' – references to the fact that, beneath the veneer of wealth and respectability, there was a world of terrible poverty, immorality and suffering. Historians who concentrate on ideas and beliefs have called it 'the Age of Ideologies', but also 'the Age of Uncertainty'.

One of your tasks, as you study the period, will be to decide for yourself the nature of the age.

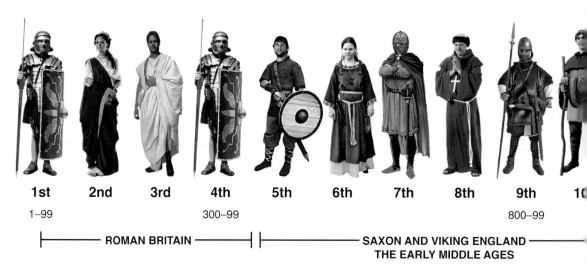

1st	2nd	3rd	4th	5th	6th	7th	8th	9th	10
1–99			300–99					800–99	

├──── ROMAN BRITAIN ────┤ ├──── SAXON AND VIKING ENGLAND ────
THE EARLY MIDDLE AGES

Activity

1 Where on the timeline would you place:
- the Norman Conquest
- the execution of Charles I
- the Great Exhibition
- the First World War?

An age of hope and glory?

The people of the time would have had much less difficulty than modern historians in finding a name which summed up the nature of their age – what they saw their time as. In 1902, the composer Edward Elgar summed up the feelings of many when he wrote his *Pomp and Circumstance* march.

The following words were set to the tune:

> *Land of Hope and Glory, Mother of the Free,*
>
> *How shall we extol thee, who are born of thee?*
>
> *Wider still and wider shall thy bounds be set;*
>
> *God, who made thee mighty, make thee mightier yet.*

As you study this book, it is unlikely that you will decide that 1745–1901 was 'the Age of Hope and Glory'! But it tells us how Elgar defined the age.

Does the timeline show all of British history?

No! People have been living in Britain for many centuries.

In 1850, a storm blew away the sand which had been covering the perfectly preserved Neolithic village of Skara Brae in the Orkneys, dating from 3000 BC. The eight houses, built all of stone, had fireplaces, beds, sideboards, seating and larders – in many respects, the people who lived there were no different from us today!

Work out how far off the edge of page 4 Skara Brae would come on the timeline.

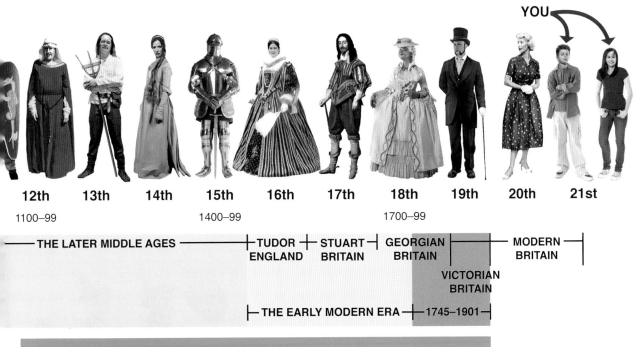

12th	13th	14th	15th	16th	17th	18th	19th	20th	21st
1100–99			1400–99			1700–99			

—— THE LATER MIDDLE AGES —— ┤TUDOR ┼ STUART ┤ GEORGIAN ├────── MODERN ┤
ENGLAND BRITAIN BRITAIN BRITAIN

VICTORIAN
BRITAIN

├— THE EARLY MODERN ERA —┼ 1745–1901 ┤

Activity

2 What made Elgar call Britain a 'Land of Hope and Glory?
3 Make a list of all the words people have applied to the period 1745–1901.
   For each word, discuss what the term implies about the period.

Meet the people of 1745–1901

The people of the Middle Ages were divided into three groups – the fighters (the king, nobles and knights), the people who prayed (priests and monks) and the people who worked (villeins and craftsmen). The statistician Gregory King divided early modern society into 'ranks and degrees' (high titles, industry, commerce, agriculture, the military and the poor). By the Victorian era, however, it was common to categorise people into three *social classes* – upper, middle and lower.

It is difficult for us today to understand how class-conscious the people of the time were. Everybody '**knew their station**', and the world was a place where a ticket inspector would not be seen socialising with a **porter**, and a **parlour maid** regarded herself as very superior to a kitchen maid.

Charles Booth

In 1896, the social researcher Charles Booth found that in London:

- 8 per cent of the people were middle and upper class
- 28 per cent were 'middle class'
- 43 per cent were comfortable working class – in regular, well-paid employment
- 16 per cent were poor – with irregular, ill-paid work
- 4 per cent were very poor, living a hand-to-mouth existence and in chronic want
- 1 per cent were 'loafers' and criminal poor.

The upper classes included the **aristocracy**, bishops, rich landowners, London gentlemen and super-rich industrialists who could buy their way into high society. They lived a life of leisure and **conspicuous expenditure** – wintering abroad, spending spring in the country and summer in London for 'the season' of balls and parties, then going to Scotland for hunting and shooting in the autumn.

The **middle classes** included rich professionals such as lawyers and doctors, and wealthy businessmen who had managed to buy their way into the local **gentry**. A middle-class father would work and earn an income, but he would live in the suburbs, employ an army of servants and send his son to one of the lesser public schools.

The **lower classes** (or 'working' classes) were divided into a strict hierarchy:

▮ On top were the skilled working classes such as **artisans**, engineers and senior clerks. They were characterised by aspiration (the hope to become middle class) and pretension (they would try to live in a 'middle class' way).

▮ Most of the lower classes, however, were labourers, who worked with their hands ten hours a day, six days a week – house servants, farm labourers, factory workers, miners, dockers and so on.

▮ The Victorians believed that there was also an underclass of paupers, criminals, alcoholics and the 'roughs'. However, investigators such as Charles Booth found out that there was a cycle of poverty for many workers. They might be well-off as single adults, or in middle age when their children were earning, but they would be poor as children, as parents with young children, and in old age.

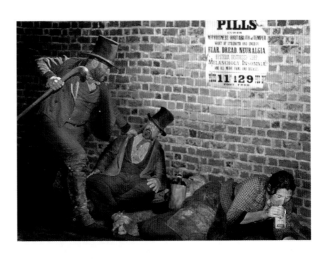

Activity

ı Present Charles Booth's figures about society in 1896, and the information about the social classes on pages 6–7, as a diagram. Discuss with a partner the best way to present the figures. You could choose a pie chart, bar graph, population pyramid or another kind of illustration for example.

Discuss your diagram with your partner, and then explain to other students what it shows about society in 1896.

A

THE BRITISH BEE HIVE

Designed in the Year 1840 by George Cruikshank and altered & etched by him.

Published by the Artist and Sold by W. Tweedie 337 Strand

Think

Why did Cruikshank represent British society as a beehive in cartoon A?

⬆ This cartoon – the British beehive – was printed by the English cartoonist George Cruikshank in 1867.

Activity

2 Working with a partner or in a small group, compare Cruikshank's 1867 cartoon above to your diagram about Victorian social classes from pages 6–7. List the similarities and differences.

3 How was George Cruikshank different from Charles Booth? How did this affect the way they portrayed British society?

4 How useful is picture A in telling us about life in nineteenth-century Britain? Share your ideas as a whole class.

Studying the period 1745–1901

What do you know about the period 1745–1901? Presumably you have heard of Queen Victoria and the Industrial Revolution, but did you know that we owe the telephone, the camera and the battery to the people of this period?

As you study the different sections of this textbook, you will discover that the period was a ground-breaking and **formative** period in British history. Here are ten of the headline events.

WATT'S STEAM ENGINE (1781)

Irish Famine (1845–52)

Abolition of the Slave Trade (1807)

Indian Mutiny (1857)

Darwin's *On the Origin of Species* (1859)

French Revolution (1789)

Great Reform Act (1832)

BATTLE OF WATERLOO (1815)

National Union of Women's Suffrage Societies (1897)

Great Exhibition (1851)

Activity

Working as a whole class:
1 Have you heard of any of the headline events listed above? Share anything you think you know about any of them.
2 List together any other things you think you know about the years 1745–1901. Sort the list into two categories:

Facts (which we can prove right or wrong)	Ideas and interpretations (which are a matter of debate and opinion)

3 How did you find out the things you know about the period – what were the sources for your knowledge (for example, books you have read)? When you have made a list, discuss for each of the items in turn: how reliable and accurate you think they are as sources for a historian?

How did the early industrialists embody the spirit of the age?

This section introduces five individuals who embodied (meaning 'represented') the spirit of the age. Through them you will gain an insight into the themes that this book will develop. As you read this section, think about what they tell us about everyday life, power, religion and Britain's international status in the late eighteenth century.

It is the 1780s and the full moon is bright in the sky. A silence is broken by the sound of horses and carriages pulling away from a mansion house outside Birmingham. Inside the building the Lunar Society is meeting – a group of like-minded individuals who meet to discuss science, industry and politics on the Monday nearest to the full moon (so there was light to travel home). Many of them were **industrialists**. They performed experiments together, shared advice and tried to understand the world that was rapidly changing around them.

⬇This painting, *An Experiment on a Bird in the Air Pump* by Joseph Wright of Derby (1768), shows the sort of experiment the Lunar Society would have done. The man in the middle is demonstrating what happens when you remove air from a jar containing a bird. The bird is about to die but the man is holding the valve ready to let air back in and revive it.

A

Activity

1 Look at the faces of the people in painting A above. What do you think they are thinking? Write thought bubbles for each.
2 What questions does this painting make you want to ask? Write a list of them.

Matthew Boulton

In the late eighteenth century, Britain was changing dramatically. What would come to be known as the Industrial Revolution was beginning in all the major cities. Birmingham was no different.

Matthew Boulton was born in 1728. His father made small decorative metal objects, like belt buckles, which were known at the time as 'toys'. Birmingham, where Boulton lived, had become known as the 'toyshop of the world'. The production of even the tiniest of these took many different processes and involved the work of lots of different people in different parts of the city.

B

↑ A view of the Soho Manufactory, 1781.

In 1759 Matthew took over the business and despite very little formal education he came up with the idea to house all production in one building, a 'manufactory'. Buying land on the outskirts of the city, he built the Soho Manufactory and designed it to look like a palace.

Housing all of the processes to produce the toys in one building meant that Boulton could develop an **assembly line** where each part of the production process was done in sequence. This sped up production drastically and meant far more items could be made. The modern factory was born.

C

Josiah Wedgwood (see page 13) said of Boulton in 1767:

'He is I believe the first or the most complete manufacturer in England in metal. He is very ingenious.'

D

In 1776 Matthew Boulton said:

'I sell here, sir, what all the world desires to have – power.'

E

◀ An example of a Birmingham 'toy'. A 1760 button – metal made by Boulton, ceramic inlay by Wedgwood.

Activity

3 What does this page show you about who had power in the late eighteenth century?
4 Do you think Matthew Boulton would have succeeded in a previous age?

2

How did the early industrialists embody the spirit of the age?

James Watt

In the eighteenth century engineering was progressing at a rapid rate. Steam engines had been invented by Thomas Newcomen (in 1712) but all they could do was pump water out of mines. They needed a genius to realise how to make them better and kick start the Industrial Revolution!

James Watt was born in 1736 in Scotland. He went to London to study musical instrument making and returned to Glasgow, building his reputation for making precise instruments. He became fascinated by steam engines. Realising that lots of energy was lost with Newcomen's engine, Watt redesigned it and made it far more powerful.

In 1775 Boulton realised the potential profit in the improved machine and invited Watt into partnership with him to produce the engines at Soho. This was very successful and the Boulton Watt Company sold engines throughout the country and even beyond (some were sold to Denmark).

Boulton realised that engines would be more useful if they could be used to power a wheel, not just pump water. Watt leapt to action and by 1784 had completed a design (picture F). Boulton Watt rotary engines were used to power a vast number of industries throughout the country including the newly expanding cotton mills in the north. The mechanisation of industry had begun.

1 Steam powers this piston to move up and down …

2 making this wheel turn using an invention by Watt called the 'sun and planet'.

F

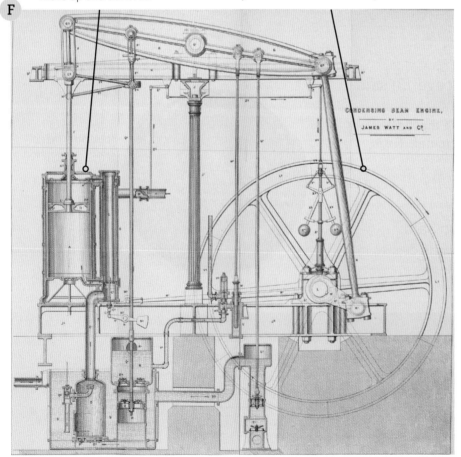

Watt's design for a rotary steam engine.

Josiah Wedgwood

Boulton and Watt were not the only successful industrialists in the Lunar Society. Josiah Wedgwood made the finest pottery Britain had ever seen.

Born in 1730, Josiah opened the world's first pottery factory in Staffordshire in 1769. Using assembly-line production, like Boulton at Soho, Wedgwood also introduced a **division of labour**, giving specific roles to individuals. This allowed them to specialise and thereby sped up the entire process.

The production of porcelain had been a Chinese secret for centuries but Wedgwood (along with others) cracked it. Experimenting for years, Wedgwood made two discoveries about how porcelain could be made. Firstly the use of Cornish china clay, and secondly a system for accurately measuring the temperature inside a kiln. For this Wedgwood was made a fellow of the **Royal Society**, the highest scientific award given at the time.

G

⬆ Trent Lock, where the Trent and Mersey Canal, River Soar and Erewash Canal form a major canal conjunction. Many members of the Lunar Society fought for the construction of canals as they allowed resources to be delivered quickly and cheaply. Wedgwood helped build the Trent and Mersey Canal, and Boulton built many others around Birmingham.

H

◀ Wedgwood was strongly opposed to slavery (see Section 3). He fought for its abolition and made medallions like this saying: 'Am I not a man and a brother?' These views came from his religious opinions – he was a member of the **Unitarian Church** which argued against slavery.

Think

Are you surprised that someone from the late eighteenth century, at the height of the slave trade, argued for its abolition?

Activity

7 How would the factory and canal system created by Boulton and Wedgwood have changed the everyday life of the people at the time?
8 What do pictures H and I reveal about the way that the world viewed Britain and the way that Britain treated the world?

I

◀ Wedgwood sold his plates around the world. His most famous set was the Green Frog service which was sold to Catherine the Great, Empress of Russia.

2

How did the early industrialists embody the spirit of the age?

Erasmus Darwin and Joseph Priestley

Not all the members of the Lunar Society were industrialists. Two of the most prominent – Erasmus Darwin and Joseph Priestley – were a doctor and a clergyman respectively. Their work and ideas reveal even more about this period.

Erasmus Darwin, the grandfather of Charles Darwin (who features in Section 4), was a **physician** in the West Midlands. Having trained at Edinburgh University, he was one of the most educated members of the Lunar Society.

Medicine was not his only interest. Darwin wrote extensively on chemistry, geology (see Source J) and botany. In chemistry he developed a system to label elements and gave names to plants that we still use today. His views on women were particularly **liberal**. He believed that women should have the same rights to education as men – a very controversial view at the time, shared only by some French philosophical thinkers.

J

Organic life beneath the shoreless waves

Was born and nursed in ocean's pearly caves …

As successive generations bloom,

New powers acquire and larger limbs assume …

Erasmus Darwin's poem 'The Temple of Nature', 1803. At this time, the Church taught that all life had been created by God, on 23 October 4004 BC.

Activity

9 Can you work out what idea Darwin was talking about in extract J (clue: his grandson Charles developed this)? What does this show about people's ideas about religion at the time?

Joseph Priestley was a **dissenting** clergyman. He ran a Unitarian Church which had very different ideas about religion from the Church of England (for example, they did not believe Jesus had a virgin birth).

Priestley is famous for his scientific discoveries. He performed extensive experiments with electricity and chemistry; he even discovered oxygen.

However, his political views were controversial. He strongly believed in **liberty** and thought the power of the government should be limited. He also strongly agreed with the French Revolutionaries, who in 1789 had overthrown their king to establish a democracy (see Section 8).

K

Yours is one of the few lives precious to mankind, and for the continuance of which every thinking man is grateful.

Thomas Jefferson, one of the founding fathers of the USA, writing to Joseph Priestley, 21 March 1801.

Activity

10 Would Darwin and Priestley's views have been tolerated in the Middle Ages or the Early Modern Era? What does this show about the late eighteenth century?

The decline of the Lunar Society

The people of Birmingham tolerated Priestley and the Dissenters (the Church most members of the Lunar Society belonged to), with their very different views, until the late 1780s. However, Dissenters were excluded from going to university or becoming politicians and they began to campaign against this in the 1780s. This angered the mainly Church of England public.

This anger grew after the **Dissenters** supported the French Revolution, which the monarchy-loving British public did not.

On 14 July 1791, the Dissenters met at the Royal Hotel to celebrate the anniversary of the French Revolution. The public had had enough and riots began. Priestley's house and many other buildings were attacked. Priestley had to flee to the USA.

James Watt wrote that the riots 'divided [Birmingham] into two parties who hate one another' and this marked the beginning of the end of the Lunar Society. Although meetings continued, the close ties between the Dissenter and non-Dissenter members were cut.

Rioters burning Priestley's house ➡ in Birmingham, 14 July 1791.

Activity

11 You have learned a lot about the men of the Lunar Society. Discuss as a whole class what their lives have shown you about everyday life, power, religion and Britain's international relations – the themes of this book – at the end of the eighteenth century.

12 Choose three of the following statements that best sum up life at the end of the eighteenth century. Find evidence from pages 10–15 to justify your decision.

13 Go back to picture A on page 10, *An Experiment on a Bird in the Air Pump*. After reading about the Lunar Society, which of the characters in the painting reflects how you feel about the end of the eighteenth century – would you have been frightened like the little girl or full of excitement like the scientist? Make sure you justify your decision.

> A time dominated by men

> A time of new opportunities

> A time when power was being shared for the first time

> A good time to live

> A time of wonder

> A time when the world was getting smaller

> A religious time

Did the Industrial Revolution have a positive impact on people's lives?

The members of the Lunar Society were not unique. In the late eighteenth century similar things were happening throughout Britain. The impact of these developments led to one of the greatest changes in the history of Britain – the Industrial Revolution. Pages 16–19 introduce the most significant parts of this revolution. Men like the members of the Lunar Society who led these changes greatly benefited from them and became very rich but was this the same for everyone else? Did this revolution have a positive impact?

Mechanisation

The work that Boulton and Watt began with their rotary engines developed throughout the nineteenth century as people realised they could use engines to power machines. This mechanisation of production meant larger quantities could be made, more cheaply, in less time.

Think

Do you think the spinning room in picture A looks like a nice place to work?

A

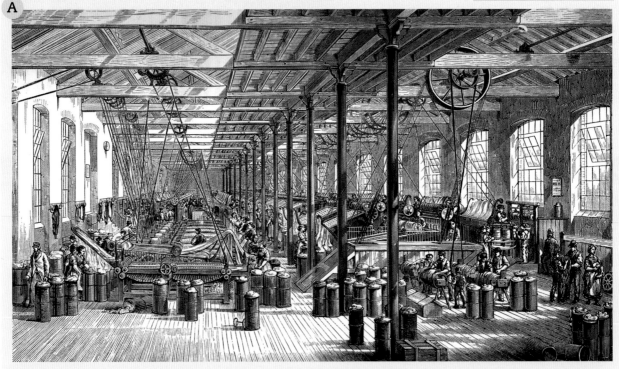

⬆ The spinning room at Shadwell Rope Works, c.1880. The vast number of machines helped to speed up the process of making the ropes which were important for shipping and hauling the goods made from industrialisation.

Activity

1 Discuss in pairs the consequences of mechanisation, urban migration, the Agricultural Revolution and steel production described on pages 16–17. Would these have been positive or negative impacts?

Urban migration

As larger factories opened, people moved from the countryside to the cities. The population in London rose by nearly 5 million between 1801 and 1901. This often resulted in cramped, poor living conditions.

◀ A photo of slums in London.

Think

What problems can you see in picture B that may have been caused by the 'boom' in city population?

Agricultural revolution

As the population rapidly increased, new techniques were needed to feed these people. Using new inventions and scientific techniques like fertilisation there was a revolution in agriculture and food was produced in far greater quantities (see table C below).

Year	Wheat	Rye	Barley	Oats	Peas/beans
1650–1699	11.36	14.19	12.48	10.82	8.39
1700–1749	13.79	14.82	15.08	12.27	10.23
1750–1799	17.26	17.87	21.88	20.90	14.19
1800–1849	23.16	19.52	25.90	28.37	17.85
1850–1899	26.69	26.18	23.82	31.36	16.30

⬆ A table showing the average amount of each crop that was able to be produced from a single acre of land in each period.

Steel production

Steel is very strong and does not rust, therefore it is a much needed metal in industry. The eighteenth-century methods of production the Lunar Society Men had relied on were not sufficient. In 1855 Henry Bessemer developed a new method which allowed it to be made quickly in vast quantities. Not only did this industry provide jobs but the metal helped in virtually all the aspects of the Industrial Revolution, notably helping to build the vast factories and railways (see page 110).

The Big Picture

2 How did the early industrialists embody the spirit of the age?

Transport

Probably one of the most obvious changes of the Industrial Revolution was in transport. George Stephenson took Watt's basic rotary engine and developed it to make some of the first locomotive trains. By the end of the nineteenth century railways covered the country and allowed fast and efficient travel. Shipbuilding was equally revolutionised. In 1843 Isambard Kingdom Brunel launched the SS *Great Britain*, the world's first iron-hulled ship driven by an engine-powered propeller.

D

⬆ *The Railway Station* by William Powell Frith, 1862. This scene depicts a busy platform at London Paddington railway station. The development of a railway network in the nineteenth century sped up communication, brought fresh food quickly into the growing towns, and allowed people to go on holiday to the seaside.

E

◀ *Launch of the* SS Great Britain *at Bristol, July 1843*, painted by Joseph Walter. Britain's huge merchant shipping fleet was the basis of its worldwide trade and a cause of the growth of its empire.

Think

What evidence can you find in pictures D and E to show what the public thought about the changes to transport?

Mining

To power the Industrial Revolution, Britain needed coal. In Wales, the Midlands and the north a vast number of coal mines opened. This provided thousands of jobs but it was very dangerous work.

F

← A photo of Blaenavon coal mine in Wales, now a World Heritage Site. The whole town of Blaenavon grew to support the mine.

Inventions

G

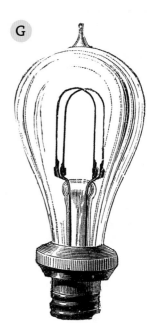

Building on the scientific and industrial principles of the Lunar Society, many inventions were discovered in the nineteenth century. Examples include the telephone, the camera, the battery and many more. These **innovations** changed people's lives.

A nineteenth-century → light bulb as invented by Thomas Edison.

> **Think**
>
> How did the telephone, camera and battery change people's lives?

Activity

2 It is important to think about the consequences of the changes we have just read about. For each change list all the consequences that you can think of.

Changes	What are the consequences of these changes?
Mechanisation	*Faster production meant more goods, produced cheaper.*
Urban migration	
Agricultural revolution	
Transport	
Mining	
Inventions	

3 Now get two coloured pens. For each consequence you have listed underline or highlight it in a different colour to show whether it is:
   a) a positive consequence
   b) a negative consequence.

4 Answer the following question:

Did the Industrial Revolution have a positive impact on people's lives?

Use all the evidence you can find on pages 10–19 in your answer.

What were the key aspects of the slave trade?

There had been slavery since ancient times but, in the eighteenth century, the British took hold of it and turned it into big business – the transatlantic slave trade.

The transatlantic slave trade was a crime against humanity. Millions of Africans – some historians claim as many as 60 million – were stolen and taken on a sea voyage in nightmare conditions to be sold in the West Indies or America.

Simplified accounts of the transatlantic slave trade call it 'the triangular trade'. Ships loaded with goods needed by Africans – such as cloth, pots, pans and guns – were taken from British slaving ports, such as Liverpool and Bristol, to 'factories' set up by Europeans on the African coast, where they were exchanged for slaves. The slaves were sailed across the Atlantic (the Middle Passage) and sold in America or the West Indies. There the ships were loaded with rum and sugar (in the West Indies) or tobacco (in America) to be sold in Britain on the ships' return.

⬇A map of the 'triangular trade', showing the route of one ship, the *Sandown*, in 1793–94. In reality, the slave trade was much more complex than this simplified picture suggests.

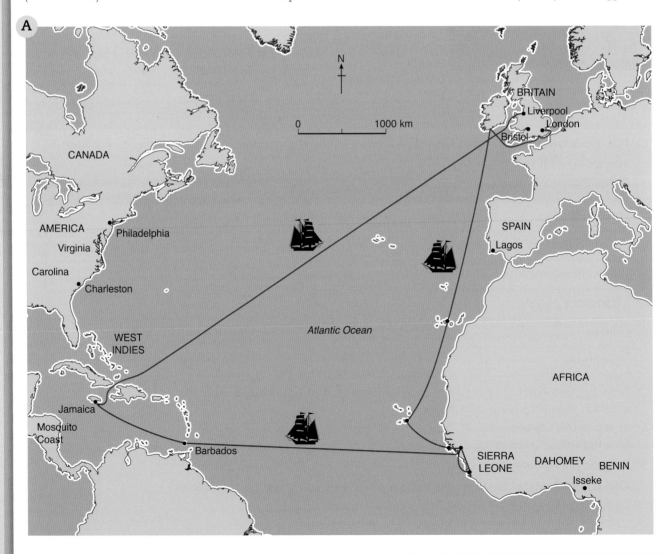

A

Important dates in the history of Britain's slave trade

1562	**1625**	**1667**
Sir John Hawkins, the English sea-captain, made his first slaving trip, capturing African slaves and selling them in the West Indies.	The British captured the West Indian island of Barbados. In 1655 they captured Jamaica. Large numbers of workers were needed for the sugar plantations, so the plantation owners started buying African slaves.	The first Black Codes were passed depriving slaves of any legal protection: plantation owners were allowed to flog their slaves to death.
1713	**1772**	**1783**
Spain gave Britain the right to sell 144,000 slaves a year to Spanish South America.	The Somerset Case: Judge Lord Mansfield ruled that, under English law, there could not be slaves in England. But this did not apply to British colonies in America or the West Indies.	The Zong case: the legal adviser Granville Sharp tried but failed to prosecute the captain of a slave ship who had thrown 133 dying slaves overboard to drown.
1787	**1788**	**1789**
The Committee for the Abolition of the Slave Trade was set up; its campaign included a sugar boycott, and Josiah Wedgwood's medallion: 'Am I not a man and a brother?' (see page 13).	William Wilberforce led the abolition campaign in Parliament. Every year he presented a bill to get the slave trade abolished; every year it failed.	Olaudah Equiano published his autobiography: *The Interesting Narrative of the Life of Olaudah Equiano, or Gustavus Vassa, The African.*
1796–1805	**1807**	**1833**
In the ten years 1796–1805, English ships took 750,000 slaves to the Americas.	Parliament passed an act abolishing the slave trade in the British Empire.	Slavery was abolished in the British Empire.

Activity

1 Working as a whole class, discuss what you can learn from pages 20–21 about:
   a) Africa at the time of the slave trade
   b) how slaves were captured and transported to the West Indies and America
   c) how slaves were treated in the West Indies and America
   d) how black Africans were treated in England.

What can Olaudah Equiano tell us about the slave trade?

In 1789, a black writer living in England published his autobiography: *The Interesting Narrative of the Life of Olaudah Equiano, or Gustavus Vassa, The African*. It was the life story of an African boy who was kidnapped, transported across the Atlantic and sold as a slave, but who later gained his freedom, became a Christian and came to live in England. In this section you are going to discover what this one man's life tells us about the slave trade in the eighteenth century.

A

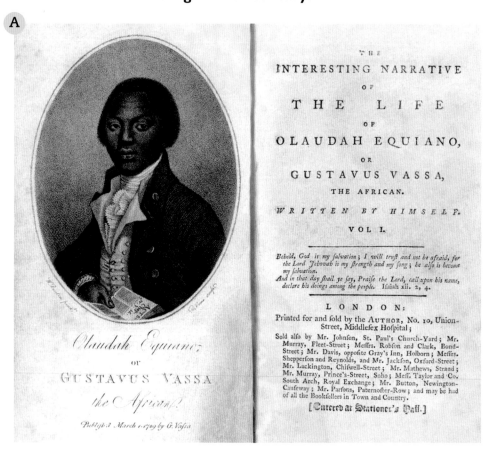

◀ The title page of Equiano's *Interesting Narrative*. Why, do you think, did the author show himself dressed as a well-to-do Englishman, holding the Bible in his hand?

In 1789, when Equiano published the *Interesting Narrative*, the campaign to abolish the slave trade was at its height.

Equiano supported the campaign. It was he who had brought the Zong case to Sharp in the first place (see page 21). Under his slave name Gustavus Vassa, with nine other black writers (who called themselves the Sons of Africa), he campaigned in the newspapers. And in 1789 – using the African name Olaudah Equiano for the first time – he wrote the *Interesting Narrative*.

After 1789, the campaign to abolish the slave trade faltered. Parliament voted to keep the slave trade and, during the political turmoil and wars of the French Revolution (see Section 8), many English people turned against all talk of 'freedom'. But Equiano organised publicity tours all over the United Kingdom and his book sold well. When he died in 1797, he was a rich man.

Think

Words change their meaning over time. In the eighteenth century, the word 'interesting' did not mean what it means today – a 1755 dictionary tells us that it meant: 'to affect; to move; to gain the affections'.

What does this suggest about Equiano's motives when writing his book?

Can we trust Equiano?

Even during his own lifetime, Equiano was accused of not telling the truth – it was claimed that he was born in the West Indies, not Africa – and, recently, some modern historians have suggested that he might have invented his African identity. Other historians, however, believe that he was clearly an African from the Igbo people of Nigeria. This page looks at Equiano's African roots.

Let's start with Equiano's own description of his childhood in extract B.

This fact is taken from the eighteenth-century American anti-slavery writer Anthony Benezet.

No one has been able to identify this place. There is an Isseke in modern Nigeria but it is only 200km from the sea. In 1788, Equiano claimed to have come from a place called Elese.

This word is similar to the Igbo word *Mgbirichi*, meaning a person who has been given facial markings.

B

That part of Africa to which the trade for slaves is carried on, extends along the coast above 3400 miles.

The kingdom of Benin … is divided into many provinces or districts: in one of the most remote and fertile of which, called Eboe, I was born, in the year 1745, in a charming fruitful valley, named Essaka. The distance of this province from the capital of Benin and the sea coast must be very considerable; for I had never heard of white men, nor of the sea … My father was one of the elders or chiefs, and was styled 'Embrenche'; a term, as I remember, of the highest distinction, signified by cutting the skin of the forehead …

I was named Olaudah, which, in our language, means 'fortunate' and having a loud voice … My father, besides many slaves, had a numerous family … In this way I grew up till I was turned the age of eleven …

The Eboe ('Igbo') are one of the peoples of modern Nigeria. In Equiano's time, however, the word just meant 'outsider', and Equiano deleted it from later editions.

The Igbo word Olaude means 'loud ring'. Ekwuno is a common Igbo family name.

At age eleven, Equiano tells us, he was kidnapped to be a slave. He was carried on 'a great many days journey … through many different countries' until, 'at the end of six or seven months', he was put on a slave ship and taken to the West Indies, and thence to Virginia in North America. There, he was sold to Mr Michael Henry Pascal, who was working as captain of a British trading ship, the *Industrious Bee*. And in this way, Equiano writes: 'It was about the beginning of the spring 1757 when I arrived in England, and I was near twelve years of age at that time.'

There are some elements of Equiano's story which we know to be untrue:

- We know, for instance, from a newspaper of the time, that the *Industrious Bee* landed in England on 14 December 1754.
- At his baptism on 9 February 1759, and again when he signed onto the ship *Racehorse* in 1773, Equiano's place of birth is listed not as Africa, but as Carolina, in North America.

Activity

2 Identify from this page five pieces of evidence that suggest that Equiano was not born in Africa. For each piece of evidence suggest an alternative explanation, which does not involve dishonesty.

3 Can you see any evidence on this page which suggests that Equiano was telling the truth and that he was born in Africa?

How did Equiano depict Africa in the *Interesting Narrative*?

Equiano began the *Interesting Narrative* with a description of the Africa from which he claimed he had been stolen. We now know that West Africa in the eighteenth century was a place of wars, famines and political chaos but historians disagree whether this helped the slave traders, or whether it was the slave trade which caused the wars, famines and political chaos. In this chapter, we will begin by studying Equiano's portrayal of Africa.

C

⬆ This racist engraving in a book written in 1763 by the English writer Archibald Dalzel shows Agonglo, King of Dahomey, throwing gifts to the crowd – goods he has procured by trading slaves. Dalzel took most of his information from an English slave trader in Dahomey, Lionel Abson (who lived there for 36 years and married a Dahomean princess). Dalzel, describing how the King of Dahomey sacrificed his prisoners of war, commented: 'Whatever evils the Slave Trade may be attended with (and there is no good without some mixture of evil) this we are sure of, it is mercy to poor wretches who would otherwise suffer from the butcher's knife'.

Historians now acknowledge that Africa before the slave trade had a developed culture and society but, in the eighteenth century, supporters of the slave trade portrayed Africans as 'ignorant and unpolished … little better than wild beasts', 'a people of beastly living, without God, law, religion or community', 'extremely lazy, full of treachery and lies and addicted to stealing'.

By contrast, Equiano gives us a very different picture of Africa:

D

We are a nation of dancers, musicians and poets … As our manners are simple, our luxuries are few [and] our cleanliness at all times is extreme … We have no strong or alcoholic drink; our main drink is palm wine …

We have also markets, at which I have been frequently with my mother. These are sometimes visited by stout mahogany-coloured men we call Oye-Eboe, which term signifies red men living at a distance … Sometimes indeed we sold slaves to them, but they were only prisoners of war, or such among us as had been convicted of kidnapping, or adultery.

Farming is our chief employment; and everyone, even the children and women, are engaged in it. Thus we are all used to work from our earliest years. Everyone contributes something to the common welfare; and as we do not know idleness, we have no beggars … The benefits of such a mode of living are obvious. The West Indian planters prefer the slaves of Benin to those of any other part of Africa, for their hardiness, intelligence, honesty and zeal … They are also remarkably cheerful. Indeed cheerfulness and friendliness are two of the leading characteristics of our nation.

As to religion, the natives believe that there is one Creator of all things … Though we had no places of public worship, we had priests and magicians … we called them Ah-affoe-way-cah. These magicians were also our doctors.

Oyibo is actually the Igbo word for a white man.

This is untrue; in fact, West Indian planters avoided Igbo slaves, regarding them as lazy and sullen.

This term contains two Igbo words: Afo meaning 'year' and cah, meaning 'announce the date'.

Activity

1 Using pages 24–25, make a list of the criticisms and accusations that white Europeans made about black Africans in the eighteenth century.
2 Using your list of accusations from Activity 1, show how Equiano was actively trying to challenge and disprove the negative European view of Africans (for example, he said they were honest, not liars).
3 Construct a grid with four headings:
   a) Africa at the time of the slave trade
   b) how slaves were captured and transported to the West Indies and America
   c) how slaves were treated in the West Indies and America
   d) how black Africans were treated in England.

   What does the *Interesting Narrative* tell us about Africa at the time of the slave trade? Add ideas from pages 24–25 to your grid. Remember to acknowledge that this is what Equiano *wanted* us to believe, and may not be wholly true.

Think

Do you believe Equiano's account of what Africa was like in Source D?

How did Equiano describe his capture into slavery?

This chapter looks at what the *Interesting Narrative* tells us about how Africans were captured and taken as slaves to the Americas.

In the *Interesting Narrative*, Equiano describes his kidnap into slavery as follows:

> One day, when all our people were gone out to their works as usual, and only I and my dear sister were left to mind the house, two men and a woman got over our walls, and in a moment seized us both, and … ran off with us.

There were two ways slave traders obtained slaves. Sometimes, they would simply capture Africans in any way they could – for example, in the way Equiano described his kidnap as a child. This was called 'lesser pillage'.

By the eighteenth century, however, the process of procuring slaves had been industrialised. The British built forts (called 'factories') on the coast. In the interior, African chiefs waged wars to capture prisoners, who were then marched to the coast and sold to the factories. This was called 'grand pillage'. In this way the slave ships could simply sail to the factories and buy their slaves in bulk.

Equiano's capture, as he described it, therefore, was unusual (though not impossible) for the time. Indeed, at that time it was fairly unusual for children to be taken as slaves at all – they were not strong enough to survive the voyage to America, and they did not sell well to planters who wanted workers, not responsibilities.

Equiano, however, had a point to make. Apologists for the slave trade – now as much as then – have argued that Africans too kept slaves and even sold their own people into slavery. Equiano's description of his six months as a slave in Africa allowed him to point out how different African slavery was to transatlantic slavery.

In Africa, slaves became members of the family – thus Equiano described how he spent a month working the bellows for a goldsmith who treated him 'extremely well', and two months as the pampered playmate of the son of a wealthy widow, so that 'their treatment of me made me forget I was a slave'. The transatlantic slave trade, by contrast, reduced human beings to 'chattel slavery', where the slaves became the 'possession' of their owner, which laid them open to barbaric treatment.

> **Think**
>
> What does picture E tell us about how slaves were transported to the West Indies and America?

E

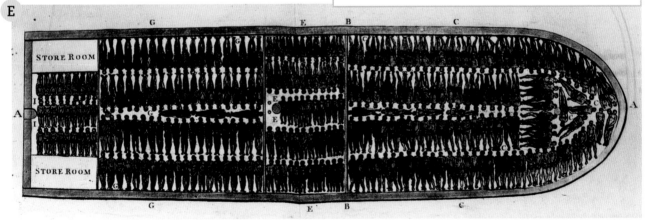

⬆ Two months before he published the *Interesting Narrative*, Equiano wrote to the *Public Advertiser* newspaper publicising this plan of the slave ship *Brookes*, which gave a space of 40cm to each adult, and 35cm to each child, for the two-to three-month voyage.

… and to the West Indies

Equiano's account gives no information about the Middle Passage that cannot be found in other accounts but that was not his intention. Rather, the *Interesting Narrative* was designed to emphasise to the reader 'the wretchedness of slavery', by describing the voyage from the point of view of a child (extract F).

F

I was carried on board [a ship called the *African Snow*] … I now thought that I had gotten into a world of bad spirits, and that they were going to kill me … When I looked round the ship too and saw a large pot boiling, and many black people chained together, every one of their faces showing dejection and sorrow, I no longer doubted of my fate … I asked if we were going to be eaten by those white men with horrible looks, red faces, and loose hair …

I now wished for the last friend, death, to save me; but soon, to my grief, two of the white men offered me eatables; and on my refusing to eat, one of them held me fast by the hands, and tied my feet, while the other flogged me severely … I feared I should be put to death, for I had never seen among any people such instances of brutal cruelty …

At last, when the ship we were in had got in all her cargo, we were all put under deck … The lack of space, and the heat of the climate, added to the number in the ship, which was so crowded that each had scarcely room to turn himself, almost suffocated us. This produced great perspirations, so that the air soon became unfit for breathing, from a variety of loathsome smells, and brought on a sickness among the slaves, of which many died, thus falling victims to the foolish greed of their purchasers. This wretched situation was made worse by the rubbing of the chains, now become unbearable; and the filth of the necessary tubs, into which the children often fell, and were almost drowned. The shrieks of the women, and the groans of the dying, made the whole a scene of horror almost unthinkable …

One day, two of my wearied countrymen who were chained together (I was near them at the time) jumped into the sea: immediately another quite dejected fellow, who, on account of his illness, was allowed to be out of irons, also followed their example … Two of the wretches were drowned, but they got the other, and afterwards flogged him unmercifully for thus preferring death to slavery. In this manner we continued to undergo more hardships than I can now tell, hardships which are inseparable from this accursed trade.

O, ye nominal Christians! might not an African ask you, learned you this from your God? Must every tender feeling be likewise sacrificed to your greed? Surely this is a new refinement in cruelty, which, while it has no advantage to justify it, thus increases distress, and adds fresh horrors even to the wretchedness of slavery.

Activity

1 Why do you think Equiano published the picture of the *Brookes* (picture E) just before he published his *Interesting Narrative*?
2 Study extract F. Make a list of the words and writing techniques Equiano uses to grab the readers' attention and gain their sympathy.
3 Debate as a class: Does it matter if Equiano was not actually himself transported on a slave ship and just synthesised an account from tales he had heard from other slaves?
4 Working in a small group, make a list of everything you can learn from pages 26–27 about how slaves were captured and transported to the West Indies and America. Add your ideas to your notes grid. Remember to acknowledge that this is what Equiano *wanted* us to believe, and may not be wholly true.

How did Equiano describe his life as a slave?

H

Slavery in the West Indies and America in the eighteenth century was particularly brutal. Modern films about slavery portray a world of back-breaking labour in the fields, punctuated by cruel punishments and vicious discrimination. This chapter examines what the *Interesting Narrative* tells us about life as a slave in the Americas.

On the *African Snow* Equiano had been given the name Michael; in Virginia he was called Jacob. In 1754, as the slave of Lieutenant Pascal, he was re-named yet again – pretentiously, Gustavus Vassa – and beaten until he accepted his new name.

For the next few years, Equiano served with Lieutenant Pascal in the British Royal Navy in the **Seven Years War**. He fought with General Wolfe in Canada, and with the British fleet which destroyed the French navy at the battle of Lagos in August 1759. During shore-leave in England, he stayed with Lieutenant Pascal's sisters – black child-slaves were the height of fashion in London – and became a Christian. He made friends and learned how to read, calculate, navigate and cut people's hair. Sailors were given prize money from ships they captured and Equiano expected at the end of the war to be allowed to buy his freedom.

Instead, on their return to port at the end of 1762, Lieutenant Pascal took Equiano's money and sold him to the captain of another ship, who, without allowing Equiano to set foot on land, sailed him back across the Atlantic and sold him to a West Indian merchant, Robert King.

⬆ The 2013 film *Twelve Years a Slave* told the story of a free black American, Solomon Northup, who was kidnapped into slavery in the mid-nineteenth century.

Northup escaped, and in 1853 wrote an account of his experiences, which has been investigated and declared accurate by modern historians.

This still from the film shows Northup working in the fields. Other scenes in the film showed him being threatened, beaten, imprisoned and lynched.

A slave in the New World

In the years 1763–66, Equiano worked as a slave for Robert King in America and the West Indies. Here is a selection of some of the things he tells us about those times in the *Interesting Narrative*:

Equiano worked for King as a clerk, stableman and hairdresser.

King 'was very charitable and humane'.

King hired Equiano out as a jobbing slave to local shipping companies – for which work Equiano was paid.

One of Equiano's jobs was to ferry new slaves recently arrived from Africa to American plantations in Virginia and Carolina.

In Carolina one gentleman offered Equiano a job as captain of one of his rice boats, but Equiano refused.

Equiano used his voyages to do a bit of trading for himself – a piece of glassware, pork, turkeys and so on – and gradually saved a sum of money.

In Charleston, Carolina, Equiano was badly beaten by a drunken local doctor, but local lawyers told him 'they could do nothing for me as I was a negro'.

Equiano often found himself cheated by white people who stole his goods or refused to pay. As a black slave, he had no protection under the law.

Equiano deplored, but could not stop, 'violent attacks upon the chastity of female slaves'.

'The overseers are indeed … human butchers, who cut and mangle the slaves in a shocking manner on the most trifling occasions, and altogether treat them in every respect like brutes.'

'I have seen a negro man staked to the ground, and cut most shockingly, and then his ears cut off bit by bit, because he had been connected with a white woman.'

In July 1766, King let Equiano buy his freedom for £40. Equiano: 'laid out above £8 of my money for a suit of superfine cloathes' and invited his friends to a dance.

Think

Equiano's description of his own experience as a slave seems to have been unfair, but not as bad as we see in modern films. Does this mean that the brutality we see in the films did not happen?

Activity

1 From pages 28–29, make a list of facts about Equiano's experiences as a slave, 1754–66. Working with a partner or in a small group, sort them into two categories:
   a) facts which reinforce the modern portrayal of slavery.
   b) facts which challenge the modern portrayal of slavery.
2 Add to your notes grid everything you have learned about how slaves were treated in the West Indies and America. Remember to acknowledge that this is what Equiano *wanted* us to believe, and may not be wholly true.

How did Equiano describe his time as a free man in England?

Black people had been living in London for many centuries, but towards the end of the eighteenth century, the numbers of black residents rose, and they began to attract racist hostility. This page studies how Equiano, in the *Interesting Narrative*, perceived his experience as a black man living in England.

In 1767, Equiano (still calling himself Gustavus Vassa) came to live in England. He eked out a living doing various business deals, working as a hairdresser, as a man-servant and as assistant to a scientist called Dr Irving.

Gradually, Equiano grew sick of London – of white people who called themselves Christians, but did not hesitate to cheat him. He asked to become a **missionary** to Africa, but was turned down.

When money ran short, Equiano signed up as a sailor, on voyages to places like Turkey, Jamaica and Spain. In 1773 he joined the *Racehorse* on a Royal Naval expedition to the Arctic. And in January 1776, with Dr Irving, he even sailed to the West Indies, bought some Africans as slaves and tried to set up a plantation on the Mosquito Coast of Central America (the project was a disaster, and in June he quit the colony).

In 1785, one of his sea voyages took Equiano to Philadelphia in America, where he was greatly impressed by the 'Free African Society', a **mutual aid organisation** for black Africans living in America. On his return to England, with a group of other Africans, he formed the Sons of Africa, who campaigned on behalf of the black community in London.

In 1786–87, Equiano worked for the government on a scheme to send former slaves to Sierra Leone in Africa. He disagreed violently with the expedition leader, Joseph Irwin, whom he eventually accused of embezzlement (for which he was dismissed). But the Sierra Leone affair had two very positive effects. Firstly, he applied for compensation for wrongful dismissal, and was given £50. And secondly – as he defended himself in the newspapers – it made him the most famous black man in England. On the back of this fame he wrote, in 1789, his bestseller – the *Interesting Narrative*.

⬆ In this 1792 cartoon, *The Rabbits*, a black street trader called Mungo (a racist stereotype), in the pose of the abolitionists' medallion (see page 13), tries to sell rotten rabbits. When the lady says 'O la how it smells', he replies: 'Misse, dat no fair – If Blacke Man take you by leg so, you smell too'.

Think

Discuss as a class all the ways in which cartoon I is offensively racist.

What does it tell us about how English people regarded black Africans at that time?

What do the historians say?

The *Interesting Narrative* gave Equiano the opportunity to help his fellow Africans *and* to make money. He married (an Englishwoman) and withdrew from public life. He died on 31 March 1797 and was forgotten until the 1960s, when historians realised that the *Interesting Narrative* was one of the first records of slavery by a slave – a fact which made it uniquely important.

Gradually, a debate has evolved about whether we can believe Equiano:

- Professor Steve Ogude (1982), from the University of Benin, denied Equiano was Igbo, and declared the *Interesting Narrative* 'fictional' – more Robinson Crusoe than truthful autobiography.
- The Nigerian historian, Catherine Acholonu (1987), found Equiano's African words to be **anglicised** Igbo; she tracked down oral historians from the village of Isseke who remembered a story about a kidnapped prince, and even located the local Ekwealou family whom, she said, looked like the portrait of Equiano.
- Vincent Carretta (2005), an American professor of English, discovered baptism and naval records that constitute 'reasonable doubt' that Equiano was born in Africa. The times demanded an African victim's account, and Equiano was 'clearly willing' to manipulate the facts.
- By contrast, Paul Lovejoy (2006), an American professor of African studies, dismissed the records as errors and asserted that the *Interesting Narrative* is 'reasonably accurate in its details'.

> **Think**
>
> 1 'The best way to read the *Interesting Narrative* is as an anti-slavery manifesto, rather than an accurate autobiography.'
>
> Debate this idea as a whole class.
>
> 2 Looking back on pages 28–31, find the things that show that Equiano was good at making money.
>
> Does the fact that the *Interesting Narrative* was a commercial venture affect your opinion of its reliability?

Activity

1 What can you learn from page 30 about the challenges and opportunities facing black people in England in the late eighteenth century? Add to your notes grid on 'how black Africans were treated in England'.

2 Use your notes grid to write an essay in four paragraphs called 'What can Olaudah Equiano tell us about the slave trade?', explaining what it tells us about:
   a) Africa at the time of the slave trade
   b) how slaves were captured and transported to the West Indies and America
   c) how slaves were treated in the West Indies and America
   d) how black Africans were treated in England.

   In your essay, pay especial attention to the times when the *Interesting Narrative* extends or challenges what we know about the slave trade.

   You must also take account of the fact that the *Interesting Narrative* may not be wholly true, so qualify your statements with words and phrases such as: 'if we believe Equiano's account ...', 'according to Equiano ...', 'apparently ...', and so on.

   Finish with a conclusion summarising your judgement.

Can you predict what happened to religion, 1745–1901?

You have probably already learned about religion and the ways in which it has had such a big effect on people's lives. These pages sum up the way that religious beliefs have changed over time and asks you to start thinking about what might have happened in the period 1745–1901.

Part 1: 1066–1509

During the Middle Ages archbishops and bishops were extremely powerful, often acting as advisers to kings. The Catholic Church was the only Christian Church throughout Europe and at its head was the Pope. He was seen as God's representative on Earth and was very powerful.

The Church taught people that they needed to pray, live a good life and follow its rules if they were to avoid Hell when they died.

The Church was extremely wealthy and owned a huge amount of land from which it collected rents. The Church also made money from the annual tithe – a ten per cent tax that everyone had to pay.

Part 2: 1509–1745

Henry VIII argued with the Pope and made himself Head of the Church in England. Although Henry was at heart a Catholic, he had set the country on the path towards becoming Protestant.

Henry's heirs (Edward, Mary and Elizabeth) had conflicting ideas about religion, which caused great unrest. Mary ordered the burning of nearly 300 Protestants while Elizabeth cracked down on Catholics who plotted against her.

The Church collected rents and tithes. Most people went to church where they were taught that the world could be understood through Christianity alone.

The Church continued to mark the milestones in people's lives – baptism, marriage and death.

By 1689, the government became more tolerant, allowing people to worship as they pleased. However, laws against Catholics were tightened throughout this period. Catholics were not allowed to become MPs or hold posts in the government or the military.

Part 3: 1745–1901

Part 4: 1901–today

Overall, there has been a slow decline in church attendance and membership. In 2013, there were 5.4 million church members in the UK, ten per cent of the adult population. This was down from twelve per cent in 2008.

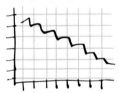

The Church of England has made some effort to keep up with changes in society. Recently the rules have been changed so that women can become vicars and bishops.

Few people continue to believe that everything written in the Bible is literally true. The majority of people, even leading Church figures, accept scientific evidence that the Earth is billions of years old and that life gradually developed and changed over time.

There has been an increase in other faiths such as Hinduism, Sikhism, Buddhism and Islam. Britain has a greater variety of religious beliefs than ever before.

Catholics no longer suffer discrimination and work in every level of society and government, including the military. The number of Roman Catholics who attend Mass has actually increased since the nineteenth century.

Activity

We have deliberately left Part 3 blank. Discuss what you think might have happened to religion in the period 1745–1901. Study the information in Parts 2 and 4 before making your predictions and be prepared to explain your thinking.

4

How far did people abandon religion in the nineteenth century?

How far did people abandon religion in the nineteenth century?

Although Britain did not have a political revolution like in France (see pages 92–110), the period 1745–1901 was a time of massive social change. Industrialisation changed the way people worked and the environment in which they lived (see pages 110–135). This helped alter people's beliefs about the world around them and how it came to be.

Religious belief in the nineteenth century played a more important part in most people's lives than it does today. However, some historians have argued that there was a crisis of faith in Victorian Britain. In this section you will weigh up how far religious belief declined.

On 30 March 1851, a religious census revealed that just 40 per cent of the population (7.25 million people) had attended church that day. To many Victorians, this seemed a disaster. Most alarmingly, working people in towns and cities did not seem interested in attending church.

Enquiry Step 1

1 What do you think the woman in picture A is thinking about? The title of the painting may give you a clue.

2 What questions does the painting make you want to ask about religion in the nineteenth century?

A

← *The Doubt*, a painting by Henry Alexander Bowler, 1855. A young woman watches two butterflies (often used as symbols for the soul) as she leans on a gravestone of a man called John Faithful. The word 'Resurgam' is carved on the stone, meaning 'I shall rise'.

B

In cities and large towns it is observable how absolutely insignificant a portion of the congregations is composed of artisans [workers] … they soon become as utter strangers to religious ordinances [ideas] as the people of a heathen country.

Horace Mann, the man who organised the Religious Census, 1851.

C

The bulk of people in humble circumstances, do not attend any place of worship … Let me not, however, be supposed to say that the great mass of the working class have no religion. Many of them have a religious feeling, of a rude and peculiar character … but which restrains them from much evil, and awakens their hopes and fears in times of suffering.

Manchester Domestic Missionary Report, 1848.

> **Think**
>
> Extracts B and C were both written about religion during the nineteenth century. What do they agree about? What do they seem to disagree about?

In 1882, another religious survey showed a further drop in church attendance. That year, the German philosopher Friedrich Nietzsche used the phrase, 'God is dead. God remains dead. And we have killed him.' Of course, Nietzsche did not mean this literally. He meant that people no longer had any need for religious belief in their lives and were turning away from faith.

Today, most historians accept that there was a decline in religious belief but would not go as far as Nietzsche. Some point out that not going to church does not mean a person has no religious beliefs. A better way of describing things might be that God was assaulted or 'roughed up' – religion declined but did not disappear.

Enquiry Step 2

Historians have suggested four factors that may have led to a decline in religious belief during the nineteenth century. We might regard these as the main 'culprits' in the assault on God. As you work through pages 36–41, you will collect evidence about each of these factors and fill in your own copy of the table below. When your table is complete, you will be able to weigh up how far each factor led to a decline in religion.

Culprit	Evidence of decline in religious belief	Evidence of continuing strength in religious belief
Industrial towns and cities		
Scientific discoveries		
New ideas (the 'Jesus of History', communism and atheism)		
The Church and other religious groups		

4

How far did people abandon religion in the nineteenth century?

Culprit 1: Industrial towns and cities

People on the move

By the 1820s, the population of Britain was increasing rapidly. New industries in coal, iron and textiles (see pages 110–135) created jobs and pulled thousands of workers from the countryside into towns and cities.

It was well known that leading Church figures, like the Archbishops of York and Canterbury, were very wealthy and this helped widen the gap between the Church and the working classes. Many working people, living in poverty and unhygienic conditions, felt that they had little in common with the Church of England. They were more concerned with where the next meal was coming from and how to pay the rent, than listening to a dull sermon.

Despite the fall in church attendance, baptisms, marriages and funerals remained an important part of people's lives. Even less well-off working-class families would lay on the most lavish religious funerals possible for their loved ones. The number of children being baptised rose in the years after 1880 and this increase continued to the end of the century.

> **Think**
>
> What does the popularity of baptisms reveal about attitudes towards the afterlife?

D

⬆ A picture showing a pew opener, 1840. The wealthier members of the congregation had the best seats or pews to sit on in church. The pew opener received a small tip for opening the gate leading to the best pews. The poorest had to sit in the less comfortable areas and so the caption reads, 'Never turns the key to th' poor.'

A 'day apart'

Even working families who did not attend church regularly regarded Sunday as a 'day apart' from the rest of the week. In the morning, while mothers prepared the most expensive meal of the week, children were sent to Sunday school for basic Christian instruction and lessons in reading and writing. Some employers even insisted that their child employees attended Sunday school. The whole family would be wearing their finest clothes or Sunday best as it was known.

> **Think**
>
> Why do you think the Church targeted the young and attached so much importance to education?

E

A Sunday school teacher with pupils, 1858. ➡ By 1888, the number of children attending Sunday school had grown dramatically with three out of four children regularly attending.

Living respectable lives

Many families owned and displayed religious artefacts and ornaments in their houses. Bibles and crucifixes were the most popular. Some households displayed pictures of Bible scenes as a reminder to live a good Christian life.

One of the bestselling books of the 1860s was a book of hymns, suggesting that religious music was popular. Another bestseller was the *Boy's Own Paper*, launched in 1878. It provided readers with a diet of adventure stories as well as a strong Christian message, highlighting the importance of clean living and honesty.

G

Britain cannot be understood without appreciating the biblical frame of mind that permeated people's lives.

Written by the historian Kenneth Morgan, *The Birth of Industrial Britain*, 2011.

F

No. 1.—Vol. I.   SATURDAY, JANUARY 18, 1879.   Price One Penny.
[ALL RIGHTS RESERVED.

MY FIRST FOOTBALL MATCH.
By an Old Boy.

IT was a proud moment in my existence when Wright, captain of our football club, came up to me in school one Friday and said, "Adams, your name is down to play in the match against Craven to-morrow."

I could have knighted him on the spot. To be one of the picked "fifteen," whose glory it was to fight the battles of their school in the Great Close, had been the leading ambition of my life—I suppose I ought to be ashamed to confess it—ever since, as a little chap of ten, I entered Parkhurst six years ago. Not a winter Saturday but had seen me either looking on at some big match, or oftener still scrimmaging about with a score or so of other juniors in a scratch game. But for a long time, do what I would, I always

seemed as far as ever from the coveted goal, and was half despairing of ever rising to win my "first fifteen cap." Latterly, however, I had noticed Wright and a few others of our best players more than once lounging about in the Little Close where we juniors used to play, evidently taking observations with an eye to business. Under the awful gaze of these heroes, need I say I exerted myself as I had never done before? What cared I for hacks or bruises, so only that I could distinguish myself in their eyes? And never was music sweeter

"Down!"

Think

What do you think Kenneth Morgan means in extract G by a 'biblical frame of mind'? Is this the same as going to church regularly?

Enquiry Step 3a

Use the information on these pages, and the discussions you had about the Think questions, to fill in the first row of your table from page 35.

◀ Front cover from the *Boy's Own Paper*, 1879.

4

How far did people abandon religion in the nineteenth century?

Culprit 2: Scientific discoveries

For hundreds of years, the Church taught that, according to the Bible, God had created the world in a single act. Some in the Church thought they could pinpoint the very moment this happened. In 1859, the Chancellor of Cambridge University declared the moment of creation was 9:00 AM on 23 October 4004 BC!

Geology and fossils

By the 1830s, several scientists had studied rocks and fossils that suggested the world had taken thousands, even millions of years to develop. These discoveries helped create doubt in the minds of many Victorians, as you can see from letter I.

H

← *Ancient Dorset*, a painting made in 1830 and based on the latest fossil finds made on the south coast of England.

I

My faith, which has never been strong, is being beaten to gold leaf ... If only those geologists would let me alone, I could do very well, but those dreadful hammers! I can hear the clink of them at the end of every cadence of Bible verse.

A letter from John Ruskin to a friend, written in 1851. Why do you think Ruskin refers to 'those dreadful hammers'?

Evolution

In 1859, Charles Darwin, a British geologist and naturalist, published his *On the Origin of Species*. He suggested that rather than being created in an instant, life had developed and changed over time – it had evolved. Evolution was driven by an automatic process which Darwin called 'natural solution'. The Church was horrified by this idea as it removed the need for a God in control of creation.

At first, the Church went on the attack. It mocked Darwin and those who supported him. However, this approach backfired. The Church ended up giving many ordinary people the idea that evolution disproved the existence of God.

By the end of the century the Church had adapted its teachings to fit alongside evolution. In 1896, Frederick Temple, a supporter of Darwin's ideas, was appointed as Archbishop of Canterbury. The Church began to argue that while evolution explained why life changed over time, it did not solve the mystery of how it began in the first place. In some people's minds, this still left room for the existence of God.

Culprit 3: New ideas

The 'Jesus of history'

During the 1830s, German and French **theologians** were writing new and controversial accounts of Jesus' life. They aimed to describe the 'Jesus of history' rather than the 'myths' they said were found in the Bible. These authors rejected the idea of miracles and the **resurrection** as superstitions and said that they were symbols rather than real events.

All of this shocked Victorian Christians who had been taught to accept everything they read in the Bible. However, such books tended to be read by middle-class intellectuals rather than large numbers of ordinary people.

Communism

Communists like Karl Marx and Friedrich Engels (see page 110) believed that the Industrial Revolution was the cause of much suffering among the working classes. They also attacked Christianity, describing religion as 'the opium of the people' – a drug that numbed people's minds to the poverty and unfairness in their lives.

Atheism

Victorian Britain also had a small but well-known minority of non-believers or atheists. They rejected religion and denied the existence of God.

The leading atheist of his day was Charles Bradlaugh (1833–91). He was elected as a Member of Parliament in 1880, but refused to swear the oath (on the Bible) that all MPs were required to make. As a result, Bradlaugh was not allowed to take his seat until the law changed in 1888. Although he had some supporters, public opinion was outraged that an atheist could even have been elected in the first place. This example shows that many Victorians regarded atheism as deeply offensive.

Enquiry Step 3b: Developing your answer

1 Use the information on scientific discoveries from page 38 to fill in the second row of your table from page 35.

2 Use the information on new ideas on this page, along with your discussions of the Think questions, to fill in the third row of your table from page 35.

J

The rich man in his castle

The poor man at his gate,

God made the high and lowly

And ordered their estate

A verse from the Victorian hymn, 'All Things Bright and Beautiful'.

Think

Why might the lyrics of the hymn in extract J have angered communists?

K

PUNCH'S FANCY PORTRAITS.—No. 48.

MR. BRADLAUGH, M.P.,
THE NORTHAMPTON CHERUB.

⬆ A *Punch* cartoon mocking Charles Bradlaugh, *Punch Magazine*, 1881.

Think

What is the attitude of the artist of picture K to Bradlaugh's atheist ideas?

4

How far did people abandon religion in the nineteenth century?

Culprit 4: The Church and other religious groups

The Church of England

At first, the Church of England had failed to keep up with the population's movement from countryside to town. It was slow in building new churches where they were most needed. As a result, even those workers who wanted to attend church often found themselves too far away.

When the Church of England finally started building new churches in the 1830s and 1840s, it came too late to attract working-class congregations.

Nonconformists

In contrast, nonconformist religious groups were quick to establish their own chapels. The biggest and most successful of these groups were the **Methodists**, who attracted large followings in Bristol, Newcastle and the East End of London. Their style of preaching was more emotional and spontaneous and could stir the passion of the crowd in a way that the Church of England failed to.

L

	1801	1851
Congregationalists	914	3,244
Baptists	652	2,789
Methodists	825	11,007

⬆ The number of nonconformist chapels, 1801–51.

Catholics

After years of **persecution** and **discrimination**, the nineteenth century finally saw some good news for Catholics. In 1829, the Catholic Emancipation Act gave them the freedom to become MPs and hold posts in the government and the military. Also, the numbers of Catholic worshippers actually increased. This was largely due to Irish Catholics moving to England to work on construction projects such as the railways.

'Saving souls' at home and abroad: The Salvation Army

In 1878, the Salvation Army was formed in the East End of London but soon spread to other towns and cities. The Salvationists preached Christian ideas and helped those living in the worst poverty. They also preached against drunkenness and even tried to persuade Parliament to pass laws restricting the sale of alcohol. Music was important to the Salvation Army and they put Christian lyrics to popular songs, played with enthusiasm by brass bands.

Despite hostility from some, by 1900 the Salvation Army had served 27 million cheap meals, lodged 11 million homeless people, traced 18,000 missing people and found jobs for 9000 unemployed people.

M

The storm raged, the wind blew, rain and snow came down. Stones were thrown, a brickbat striking the head of Sergeant Fellowes, breaking his head, and causing the loss of a pint of blood. He was taken to the hospital, had his head bandaged, and came back leaping and praising God.

An extract from *War Cry*, the Salvation Army Journal, 1880s.

Think

Why might some working people in the cities have acted with hostility towards the Salvationists as described in extract M?

Missionaries

As the British Empire expanded and explorers penetrated into unmapped areas of the world, missionaries believed it was their job to 'shine the light' of Christianity on the people there. Many missionaries viewed native customs as **barbaric** and ignorant. They felt it was their religious duty to help spread the 'Three Cs' – Christianity, commerce and civilisation.

During the nineteenth century, thousands of missionaries could be found across the globe, working hard to convert the locals. By 1900, there were 41 million Christians in Africa, Asia and the Pacific. However, many converts did not remain Christian in the long term. Others adapted Christianity to fit around their own customs, traditions and beliefs – even practising rituals that the missionaries disapproved of.

> ### Think
>
> How does the artist who painted picture N give the impression that Livingstone is superior to the Africans around him?

Enquiry Step 3c: Developing your answer

Use the information on the 'Church and other religious groups' on pages 40–41 to fill in the final row of your table from page 35.

⬆ David Livingstone in the African continent. The painting is entitled 'Livingstone: His Message.' The explorer and missionary did much to increase our geographical understanding of Africa. However, he was less successful when it came to converting Africans to Christianity.

Enquiry Step 4: Concluding your enquiry

It is time to use the work you have done in Enquiry Steps 1–3 to answer the enquiry question: How far did people abandon religion in the nineteenth century?

1 Use your completed tables to decide which of the culprits (factors) did the most damage to religious belief and faith. Arrange the culprits from the least to the most damaging. Be prepared to discuss your decision with the rest of your class.

Minor damage   Some damage   Serious damage

2 Write your final answer to the enquiry question. You can use the statements below to help you structure it.

> On the one hand, there is evidence of a decline in religion during the nineteenth century … (Give evidence from your table and explain what this shows.)

> On the other hand, religion remained strong during the nineteenth century … (Give evidence from your table and explain what this shows.)

> Overall, I think … (Make a decision – was religion in serious decline or still strong in nineteenth-century society? Don't sit on the fence!)

How democratic was the United Kingdom by 1901?

England's Parliament began in the Middle Ages, and grew steadily in power. In the seventeenth century, Parliament went to war to prevent the king retaking absolute power. In this section you will collect information about how Britain's *parliamentary* government of 1745 gradually became more *democratic* as time went on, and you will finish by evaluating how democratic the United Kingdom had become by 1901.

Today, if you were not born in Britain and want to become a UK citizen, you have to take an exam to prove you know and understand about Britain. The study materials for the exam on the development of British democracy start with the following statement:

Democracy is a system of government where the whole adult population gets a say. At the turn of the nineteenth century, Britain was not a democracy as we know it today. Although there were elections to select Members of Parliament (MPs), only a small group of people could vote. They were men who were over 21 years of age and who owned a certain amount of property.

Life in the United Kingdom Test Study Materials (2014).

How democratic was the UK government in 1800?

To say that the UK government in 1800 'was not a democracy' is, in fact, an understatement. Today, we would condemn such a government as **corrupt** and **repressive**.

Out of a population of 10 million people, only 250,000 men (five per cent of the adult population) were allowed to vote. Women could not vote. Huge new towns like Birmingham and Manchester had no MPs, yet 'rotten boroughs' – places which had been important in the Middle Ages but by 1800 had shrunk to tiny villages – returned two MPs.

Parliament did not represent all people; it represented the rich. Many elections to Parliament were controlled by the local landowner, who simply told the voters how to vote – in the 1802 general election, out of 243 **constituencies**, there were only 73 contested elections. Once in Parliament, the government gave MPs bribes and easy, well-paid official jobs to buy their support.

Terrified by the French Revolution (see Section 8) the government clamped down on all political activity:

- In 1799 the Combination Act stopped people forming a **trade union**.
- In 1817 the government suspended *Habeas Corpus* (the law which prevented people being imprisoned without a trial).
- In 1819 the government passed the Six Acts. These were designed to stop people holding meetings or writing anything critical of the government. They also gave the government the right to search people's houses for weapons.

When a crowd gathered at St Peter's Fields in Manchester in 1819 to demand reform, the authorities sent in the cavalry. Eleven people were killed and the event became known as the Peterloo Massacre (a satirical reference to the victory over Napoleon at Waterloo in 1815).

A

Think

In what different ways are the two rival candidates in picture A trying to win votes? Which ways would be illegal nowadays?

Before 1872, elections were held in public, so everyone could see who people were voting for. Candidates bribed and bullied the voters; some elections degenerated into a small local war between rival candidates. Hogarth's *Election Dinner* was inspired by a particularly corrupt election in 1754. Can you spot the following in the picture:

- the candidate being forced to kiss a very ugly woman
- a dealer, 'Abel Squat', packing up gloves, ribbons and stockings to send as gifts to voters
- the alderman who has eaten so many oysters he has collapsed and is being **bled** by a doctor
- the honest doctor trying to refuse a bribe, and his wife mocking him for doing so
- a butcher rubbing gin into the wound of one of the thugs the candidate has hired to attack his opponent
- the prostitute whom the candidate has hired to 'entertain' his guests
- a procession in favour of the rival candidate taking place outside the window?

Activity

1 Using pages 42–43, list all the ways the UK's government in 1800 was far from democratic.
2 Start a collection of factual information by making a list of the key events / dates you have learned about Britain's government in 1800.

How did the franchise grow in the nineteenth century?

In this chapter you will continue your collection of factual information about the growth of British democracy and begin to think about how democratic the United Kingdom had become.

The *Life in the United Kingdom Test* sees the nineteenth century as the key moment in the development of Britain's democracy:

> The franchise (that is, the number of people who had the right to vote) grew over the course of the nineteenth century and political parties began to involve ordinary men and women as members.

During the eighteenth century, two rival political parties had developed in Parliament:

- the Tories, who represented the landowners and wanted to turn back the clock
- the Whigs, who represented the new business classes.

Neither party wanted to reform the system, which gave and protected their seats in Parliament. In 1830, however, a wave of revolutions swept across Europe, and the Whigs became convinced that – if Parliament was not reformed – there would be a revolution in England too.

Think

How does picture A give the impression that the Great Reform Act of 1832 was a great step forward for democracy in Britain?

A

↑ This 1831 drawing shows the Whigs attacking the old rotten system of voting, while the Tories try to save it. At its base are toadstools (a symbol of corruption) and vipers (a symbol of repression), and in its branches are the 'rotten boroughs' which gave a safe seat in Parliament to some MPs (represented by cormorants – greedy birds). In the distance, the king and queen, and figures representing England, Ireland and Scotland, cheer on the reformers. Can you spot Lord Grey, the Whigs' leader?

In the nineteenth century, therefore, four key acts were passed to reform the voting system.

The 1832 Reform Act

In 1831, the Whigs passed a reform bill through the House of Commons; it was defeated in the House of Lords. The Whigs asked the King to create 50 new lords to get the bill through the Lords; the King refused. There were riots in Nottingham, Derby and Bristol, the Lords gave way and passed the bill.

The Act:
- abolished the old rotten boroughs, and gave MPs to 43 towns
- gave the vote to all men with land worth more than £10 a year
- increased the electorate to 650,000 men (six per cent of the adult population).

The 1867 Reform Act

After a reform rally in Hyde Park in 1866 degenerated into rioting, the Tory Prime Minister, Benjamin Disraeli, steered a reform bill through Parliament
The Act:
- gave more MPs to the growing industrial areas of the north of England
- gave the vote to all male urban householders who paid rent of more than £10 (£12 in rural areas)
- increased the electorate to 2.5 million men (fifteen per cent of the adult population).

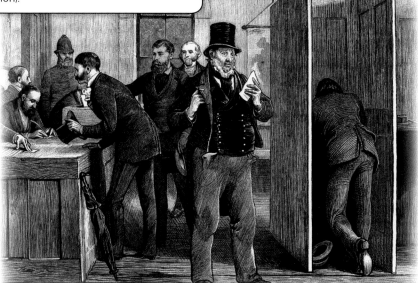

The 1872 Ballot Act

A large electorate made it impossible to bribe voters, but it was still possible to bully them, and elections were violent affairs. In 1872, therefore, the government passed the Ballot Act, which made voting secret.

As a result, both political parties had to modernise. They set up local branches to gather local support. In 1880 the Whig leader William Gladstone invented modern campaigning when he made a tour (known as the Midlothian campaign) giving speeches which were then reported in newspapers.

The 1884 Reform Acts

In 1884, the House of Commons, which wanted further reform, negotiated a compromise with the House of Lords (which did not).

These Acts:
- set up a Boundary Commission to try to ensure that constituencies had equal numbers of voters
- increased the electorate to 5.5 million men (30 per cent of the adult population).

Activity

1. Draw pie graphs showing the percentage of the population which had the vote in the general elections of 1802 (see page 42), 1835, 1868 and 1885.
2. Discuss as a whole class:
   a) Does the 1832 Act deserve to be called the 'Great Reform Act'?
   b) The modern historian Edgar Feuchtwanger said that the 1884 Act 'moved the country almost all the way towards political democracy'. Do you agree?
3. Continue your collection of factual information by making a list of the key people and the events/dates you have learned about in this chapter.

How did Chartism affect Britain's developing democracy?

The *Life in the United Kingdom Test* sees a group called the Chartists as the turning point for British democracy. This chapter looks at the Chartist movement, and asks you to assess its role in the development of British democracy.

In the 1830s and 1840s, a group called the Chartists campaigned for reform. They wanted six changes, which they called 'the Charter' or 'the Six Points':

1 Every man to have the vote
2 Elections every year
3 All regions to be equal in the electoral system
4 Secret ballots
5 Any man to be able to stand as an MP
6 MPs to be paid.

At the time, the campaign was generally seen as a failure. However, by 1918 most of these reforms had been adopted.

Chartism grew out of working class anger that the 1832 Reform Act did not give them the vote. In 1836 a group of working men founded the London Working Men's Association (LWMA) to lobby Parliament to change the voting laws. In 1838 they published 'The Charter'.

The LWMA hoped to use moral arguments and peaceful methods. At the same time, however, campaigners in the north of England, led by an Irish journalist called Feargus O'Connor, had a different view. They *demanded* the Six Points and threatened physical force if they did not get their way. For them, the vote was not an end in itself – it was a way to get a Parliament which would pass laws which would give them a better standard of living (see extract A).

The first petition

The Chartists were brilliantly organised. They set up branches in many towns. O'Connor published a newspaper called *The Northern Star* which kept them all informed. In 1839 they were able to present a petition asking Parliament to accept the Charter. It contained 1.3 million signatures. Parliament debated it, and rejected it by 235 votes to 46.

There was an outburst of strikes and riots. In Wales, more than 1,000 miners led by John Frost marched on Newport and had to be dispersed in a short battle – 22 Chartists were killed.

A

The question of Universal Suffrage is a knife and fork question. Every working man has a right to a good coat on his back, a good roof for the shelter of his household, a good dinner upon his table, no more work than will keep him in the enjoyment of plenty, and all the blessings of life that reasonable men could desire.

JR Stephens, a Methodist minister and Chartist leader, speaking at a rally in Manchester in 1838. By 'Universal Suffrage' Stephens meant the demand for every man to have the vote.

B

Fools! We have the physical force, not they.

Sir Charles Napier, commander of the government troops in the north of England, wrote this in his diary in 1839. He sympathised with the Chartists and begged O'Connor not to use physical force.

The second petition

In 1842 a second petition, with 3 million signatures, was presented to Parliament, which rejected it by 287 votes to 49.

This time, the rejection was followed by a wave of industrial sabotage called the Plug Plots. Chartists broke into factories and wrecked the machinery, including taking out the plugs from the boilers of steam engines. Troops were sent to enforce law and order and many Chartist leaders were arrested.

This 1848 cartoon in the humorous magazine ➡ *Punch* mocks a 'physical force' Chartist getting ready to rebel.

The third petition

In 1848 a third petition, claiming more than 5 million signatures, was taken to Parliament, which found that the petition actually had fewer than
2 million signatures, many of them fake – including 'Queen Victoria', the former Prime Ministers 'Robert Peel' and the 'Duke of Wellington', and people signing 'Cheeks the Marine', 'Pugnose' and 'Long Nose'. MPs refused to debate the petition.

A rebellion was planned, but police spies had infiltrated the organisation, and the plotters were arrested and transported.

This cartoon in the magazine *Punch* mocks the ➡ 1848 petition. The figure to the left of the young Queen Victoria is Robert Peel; and that to her right is Mr Punch, behind whom stands the Duke of Wellington.

Activity

1 Discuss as a whole class:
   a) What is the connection between extract B and picture C?
   b) Do pictures C and D prove that the government was not frightened of Chartism?
2 Working in a small group, gather all the evidence on pages 46–47 which tells you what sort of people joined the Chartist campaign. Was the Chartist movement 'revolutionary'?

Did the Chartists fail?

After 1848, writes the historian Simon Mason, Chartism was 'laughed out of existence'. O'Connor went insane, and the last meeting, held in 1858, was attended by only a handful of people.

Many historians, however, have argued that, although it was a failure in the short term, in the long term the Chartist movement achieved its aim and changed politics.

E

However, since 1848, five of the six points of the Charter have become law:

1 Reform Acts in 1867, 1884 and 1918 gave more adult males the vote.
2 In 1872 the Ballot Act introduced secret voting.
3 In 1911 MPs received payment for their work.
4 In 1884 a redistribution of parliamentary seats led to constituencies of equal sizes.
5 In 1874 Parliament abolished the property qualification for MPs.

Simon Mason, *Work Out Social and Economic History*, published in 1988.

F

In 1839 and 1842 the House of Commons, even though it voted to reject the Chartist petitions, nevertheless debated the issue of the Charter and its demands [and] sure enough, by the 1850s reform was back on the agenda again ...

Secondly, Chartism was of undoubted importance as a model of how a working-class movement might operate ... In 1844, when Chartism seemed dead after the failure of the 1842 petition, a group of former Chartists in Rochdale set up a co-operative society which became a model for similar movements around the world ... The unions of the 1850s and 1860s, known as New Model Unions, owed much to Chartism in terms of their organisation, methods, and in many cases their membership.

Sean Lang, *Parliamentary Reform 1785–1928*, published in 1999.

Activity

3 Discuss as a whole class the role of Chartism in the development of British democracy in the nineteenth century:
   a) Many historians claim that, although Chartism failed in the short term, it won in the end. Do you agree? Or was Chartism just a failure?
   b) What does the story of Chartism tells us about British democracy in the middle of the nineteenth century?

G

↑ A contemporary engraving of an Anti-Corn Law League demonstration.

H

We have had our meetings of ministers, we have obtained the co-operation of the ladies, we have resorted to tea-parties and taken those peaceful means of carrying out our views, which mark us rather as a middle-class set of agitators.

Richard Cobden, speaking in 1842 to an Anti-Corn Law League meeting.

Postscript – the Anti-Corn Law League

In 1819, at Peterloo, the authorities set the troops on the demonstrators. The government ignored, ridiculed and set the troops on the Chartists too. But it would be wrong to represent Parliament in the nineteenth century as blind to the needs of the people or deaf to public demands for reform.

A successful campaign

One example of a successful political campaign would be the Anti-Corn Law League.

In 1815, to protect British agriculture, the government passed the Corn Laws, which forbade the import of foreign wheat until the price in Britain was £4 a **quarter**. This annoyed British businessmen. They believed in **laissez-faire** – that trade should be allowed to be conducted without any interference – and they said that expensive wheat (and therefore bread) forced up wages and harmed business. In 1838 Richard Cobden and John Bright, two Lancashire manufacturers, began a campaign to get the Corn Laws repealed.

The Anti-Corn Law League was opposed by powerful landowners but in 1846 there was a famine in Ireland and Prime Minister Robert Peel steered through legislation to abolish the Corn Laws – even though it ruined his political career.

Activity

4 Working in a small group, gather all the evidence on page 49 which tells you what sort of people joined the Anti-Corn Law campaign. Was the Anti-Corn Law League 'revolutionary'?
5 Discuss as a whole class: Why did the Anti-Corn Law League succeed, but the Chartists fail?
6 Continue your collection of factual information by making a list of the key people, and the events / dates you have learned about in this chapter on Chartism and the Anti-Corn Law League.

How and when did the working classes find their voice?

You saw on pages 44–45 that, even by 1901, the majority of people did not have the vote. But democracy is about much more than simply the right to vote – it is about having a say in the way you are governed. On pages 46–49 you saw that, in the middle of the nineteenth century, the right to be heard was restricted to the middle classes; the working classes were ignored, ridiculed and – when they tried to protest – attacked.

This chapter looks at how and when the working classes found their voice.

Think

Why did scenes like the one in picture A frighten the government – what might the ranks and banners remind them of?

The early trade unions

The Combination Acts were repealed in 1824, and trade unions became legal, but they still struggled to have any effect. Attempts at huge unions such as the National Association for the Protection of Labour (1830–32) and the Grand National Consolidated Trades Union (1834–35) quickly collapsed. Employers sacked workers who joined a union, and **blacklisted** them so that they could never get a job anywhere. In 1834, the Tolpuddle Martyrs – six Dorset farm workers who had tried to form a union – were convicted of taking a secret oath and transported to Australia.

A

⬆ A GNCTU rally in Copenhagen Fields, Islington, London, in 1834, protesting against the treatment of the Tolpuddle Martyrs.

The new model unions

In the 1850s, however, skilled workers began to form successful unions such as the Amalgamated Society of Engineers (the ASE). Instead of agitation, they focused on education, professional standards and providing their members with benefits in case of accident or illness (see extract B and picture C).

The new unions

Eventually, unskilled workers formed unions too. From 1868 they united to form the Trades Union Congress (TUC). They lobbied MPs and got laws passed which allowed peaceful **picketing**. They concentrated on action to improve their members' pay and conditions of work. By 1901, more than 2 million people were members of a union.

In 1888 the women in the Bryant and May match factory held a successful strike for better pay and conditions, and in 1889 the London Dockers held a five-week strike which forced their employers to agree guaranteed work and a minimum hourly wage. Both the match girls and the dockers had considerable public sympathy.

B

He must be healthy, have worked for five years at the trade, be a good workman, of steady habits, of good moral character, and not more than 45 years of age.

Terms for the admission of new members issued by the Amalgamated Society of Engineers, 1862.

C

The dove of peace oversees the whole scene.

The goddess Fame, standing on a horn of plenty, gives laurel wreaths to a blacksmith and an engineer.

The blacksmith refuses to mend the sword of Mars, the god of war.

Clio, the goddess of history, gives the engineer a design.

Two figures illustrate the fable of the sticks, showing that unity is strength.

Three cameos show Samuel Crompton (inventor of the spinning mule), James Watt (improver of the steam engine) and Richard Arkwright (inventor of the spinning frame).

A phoenix rises from the ashes.

In the building are scenes of industry, outside are the results of their work.

The thistle, rose and shamrock represent Scotland, England and Ireland.

◀ Each member of the ASE was given a hand-coloured membership certificate.

The Labour Party

In 1892 a Scottish miner called Keir Hardie was elected for Parliament in West Ham, in London. Next year he formed the Independent Labour Party. By the end of the century, workers' leaders were beginning to realise that they needed a political voice, as well as union representation. In 1900, therefore, the TUC agreed to form a Labour Representation Committee, which in the 1900 election managed to win two seats in Parliament. In 1900 it won 29 seats, and changed its name to the Labour Party. But the Party had to wait until 1924 for the first Labour Prime Minister.

> **Think**
>
> Study picture C. What can we learn from its symbolism about the attitudes and beliefs of the union?

Activity

1 Working in a small group, gather all the evidence on pages 50–51 which explains why the new model unions were accepted by the government and middle classes.
2 Discuss as a whole class: When and how much of a voice did the working class gain by 1901 in the way they were governed? Explain and justify your suggestions.
3 Continue your collection of factual information by making a list of the key people and the events / dates you have learned about in this chapter.

How did changes in local government affect the development of British democracy?

In the same way that democracy is about more than just the vote (as you saw on pages 50–51), so government is about more than just laws made in Parliament. The Victorians invented local government and this chapter investigates how this affected people, especially those who lived in towns.

Before the Victorians, there were no local councils as we have today. In the towns and cities, civic bodies – with titles such as the 'commission' or the 'vestry' – struggled to light the streets, organise the **Night Watch** and clean the streets. As the towns grew, these bodies proved increasingly not up to the task, and the poorer areas of many early nineteenth-century towns became dark, lawless slums which swam with sewage.

⬇A cartoon from 1828 suggesting that the only thing vestry members were interested in was a good meal at the ratepayers' expense.

The invention of local government

The Victorians realised that as well as a Parliament to make the laws, they needed efficient government at local level.

In 1835, therefore, the Municipal Corporations Act allowed towns to apply to become Corporations, with a Council elected by ratepayers. The Local Government Act of 1888 took this further, setting up County and Borough Councils to take charge of local government. By the end of the century, local councils had been given control or influence over a vast range of services and functions (see picture C). Local councils vied with each other to build the biggest reservoirs, or the most impressive museum.

Joseph Chamberlain (who became mayor at the young age of 37) made Birmingham famous as 'the best governed city in the world'. The council bought the local gasworks and the local waterworks and cleared and rebuilt large areas of slums. It built libraries, swimming pools and a museum and art gallery. It was said that, after just three years as mayor, Chamberlain left the town 'parked, paved, marketed, gas and watered, and improved'.

A

B

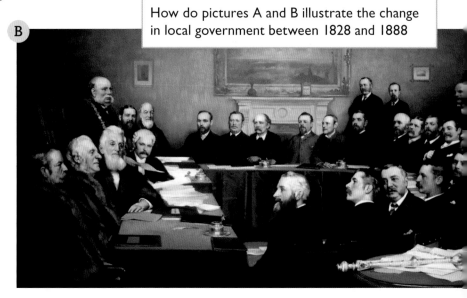

A meeting of Hartlepool ➡ Borough Council in 1888.

> **Think**
>
> How do pictures A and B illustrate the change in local government between 1828 and 1888

C

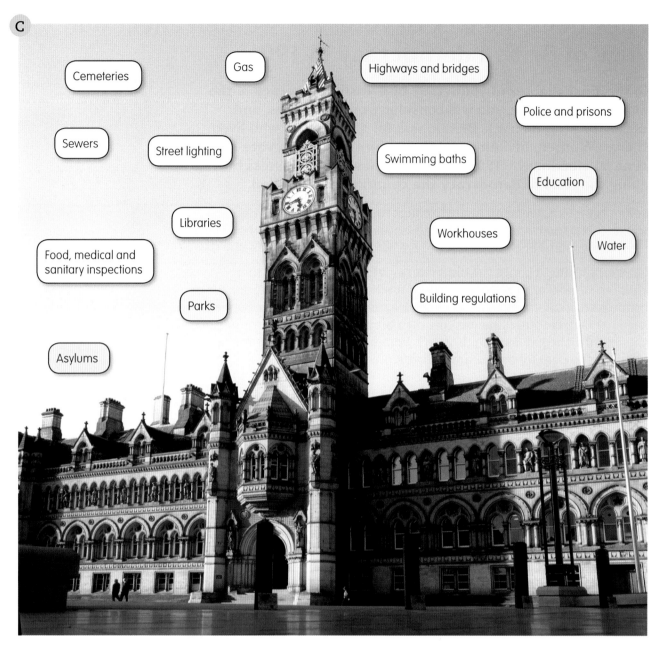

Cemeteries

Gas

Highways and bridges

Police and prisons

Sewers

Street lighting

Swimming baths

Education

Libraries

Workhouses

Water

Food, medical and sanitary inspections

Parks

Building regulations

Asylums

A ratepayers' democracy

Because councillors were unpaid, the city and town councils tended to be dominated by rich landowners and manufacturers.

But there was great interest in local matters, and most people were educated enough to be able to read the local newspapers. All householders and small shopkeepers paid rates and had the vote and, after 1869, women had the vote in local elections too. After 1894, women were allowed to sit on local councils, leading some historians to declare Britain's system of local government by the end of the nineteenth century 'a ratepayers' democracy'.

⬆ Some council responsibilities by the end of the nineteenth century; the building is Bradford Town Hall, built in 1873.

Activity

1 Councils had many responsibilities by 1901, and there were many examples of civic pride, but does this amount to 'a ratepayers' democracy'? What does your class think?
2 Continue your collection of factual information by making a list of the key people and the events / dates you have learned about in this chapter.

How does the lack of votes for women affect our view of British democracy in 1901?

In this final chapter of your study of British democracy in the nineteenth century, you will consider women's rights, and decide how democratic Britain was for the women who lived there. Women, of course, had not won the right to vote in general elections by 1901, but your task will be to assess how far along the road to democracy the country had travelled.

Before the 1840s, women did not just lack the vote, they lacked human rights. A married woman was the possession of her husband, who had the right to beat her, throw her out or refuse her access to the children.

Gradually, things changed. Women were given the right to see their children in 1839 and the right to seek a divorce (if her husband beat her or committed adultery) in 1857. After 1882 a married woman was allowed to keep her own earnings and own her own property. However, for most of the century, the key issue for Britain's women was not so much the right to vote, but the fight for basic human rights.

Votes for women

Nevertheless, votes for women had been brought up by the writer Mary Wollstonecraft in 1792, and the MP and reformer John Stuart Mill had tried to get it into Disraeli's 1867 Reform Act. In 1869, women ratepayers were given the vote in local elections.

After 1870, MPs debated, and rejected, a Women's Voting Bill almost every year. There were women's suffrage societies in most of the big towns and, in 1897, a campaigner called Millicent Fawcett united these societies into the NUWSS (the National Union of Women's Suffrage Societies). It had 50,000 members, most of them middle class and well educated. The Suffragists, as they were called, collected petitions, lobbied MPs, went on speaking tours and held debates and meetings.

By 1901, they had got … nowhere. Not until 1918 were women over 30 given the vote (and women over 21 were not given the vote until 1928).

A

⬆ Opponents of women's suffrage argued that politics was not in the 'women's sphere' – which meant the home and family. This 1884 cartoon in the humorous magazine *Punch* – entitled 'A Troubled Dream of the Future' – mocks the type of women who might want to end up in Parliament.

Think

How did the cartoonist who drew picture A seek to ridicule women's suffrage? (Blue stocking – see her knitting – was a name used for an educated female.)

B

Think

Why has the cartoonist of picture B depicted the Suffragists so differently from the women and child who are watching them?

⬆ This 1870 *Punch* cartoon shows Lydia Becker and other Suffragists hammering on the door of Parliament demanding votes and rights. (Lydia Becker was editor of the *Women's Suffrage Journal*, in which she argued that there was no difference between men and women.)

Think

What can a historian infer from picture B about the progress women's suffrage had made by 1870?

Activity

1 Discuss as a whole class: As far as women's suffrage is concerned, how far along the road to democracy had Britain progressed by 1901? Explain and justify your suggestions.

2 Continue your collection of factual information by making a list of the key people and the events / dates you have learned about in this chapter.

Pulling it all together: How democratic was Britain by 1901?

When you started studying this topic you could have been forgiven for thinking that it was a simple 'yes' or 'no' question: 'did Britain have universal adult suffrage?', and that the answer was 'No'. In that respect, Britain is not even the world's first democracy. The Isle of Man introduced full adult suffrage in 1881 and New Zealand in 1893, so they both beat Britain by decades.

However, by now, you should have realised that democracy is not just about having a vote: it is about having a say. And it is clear that, although British people did not get full adult suffrage until 1928, they clearly had much more of a say in 1901 than they had in 1800.

So now it is time to organise your thoughts about how democratic Britain was by 1901.

Activity

Moments in British democracy

1 The Post Office often issues sets of stamps – such as a 2008 set celebrating women of distinction – but it has never issued a set of stamps commemorating the growth of British democracy in the nineteenth century.

You are going to rectify that omission. Looking back through your notes on pages 42–55, work in a group to choose a set of twelve stamps comprising

▌ the four most important people

▌ the four most important events / dates

▌ the four most important issues

in the growth of democracy, 1800–1901. Focus on choosing the people and developments which were most effective in *changing* Britain's system of government into a democracy.

2 Mock up a rough design of your stamps. Compare your selection with other groups. Did you choose the same people, events and issues? Explain and debate who made the best choices.

The *Life in the United Kingdom Test*: the development of British democracy

We began this section by telling you about the *Life in the United Kingdom Test*, which you have to take if you were not born in Britain and want to become a UK citizen. As you have studied this topic, you have learned that the Study Materials for the test:

a started by defining democracy as 'a system of government where the whole adult population gets a say' (see page 42)

b acknowledged that in 1800 Britain was not a democracy (see page 42)

c claimed that the number of people who had the vote grew during the nineteenth century, and that people became more involved in politics (see page 44)

d credited the Chartists with being the turning point (see page 46)

e finished the story with a date outside your study period – 1918 (see page 46).

Activity

The development of British democracy

3 Working in a small group, discuss the development of democracy outlined in points a–e above.

▌ Are there any claims with which you agree?

▌ Are there any claims with which you disagree?

▌ Are there any important people, events or issues which the *Life in the UK Test* has left out?

Explain your reasoning and give facts which prove your judgements.

4 Working alone, write your own version of the *Life in the United Kingdom Test Study Materials*, which will give a better interpretation of the development of British democracy in the nineteenth century.

Write it in about 250 words, in five paragraphs, which will describe and explain:

a) What is your definition of 'democracy'?

b) What was the government of Britain like in 1800?

c) How did Britain's democracy develop and grow in the nineteenth century?

d) Who, or what developments, seem to have caused those changes in Britain's government?

e) How democratic do you judge Britain to have been by 1901?

Throughout, remember to explain your reasoning and give facts to prove your judgements.

How important was the Great Hunger in the breakdown of England's relationship with Ireland?

How important was the Great Hunger in the breakdown of England's relationship with Ireland?

From 1541, when Henry VIII declared himself King of Ireland, England had ruled Ireland but they were not unified as one state. In 1798 a failed Irish rebellion convinced the English government that the countries should be united with one Parliament and one Church. Thus, in 1801 the *Act of Union* created The United Kingdom of Great Britain and Ireland. This was not an easy relationship. After a turbulent hundred years, the Irish rebelled in 1916 (again wanting independence from Britain) and 1921 saw the break-up of the union.

This section looks at the relationship between England and Ireland in the century following their union and at the underlying causes of the complete breakdown of the relationship by 1921.

In this chapter you will investigate the events of these years (1801–1920), from the Act of Union to the partition. In doing so, you will attempt to answer the big question 'How important was the Great Hunger in the breakdown of England's relationship with Ireland?' Before we do that, however, we need to develop an overview of Irish history.

A

THE KINDEST CUT OF ALL.

WELSH WIZARD. "I NOW PROCEED TO CUT THIS MAP INTO TWO PARTS AND PLACE THEM IN THE HAT. AFTER A SUITABLE INTERVAL THEY WILL BE FOUND TO HAVE COME TOGETHER OF THEIR OWN ACCORD—(ASIDE)—AT LEAST LET'S HOPE SO; I'VE NEVER DONE THIS TRICK BEFORE."

This cartoon from *Punch* in 1920 is called 'The Kindest Cut of All'. The cartoon is commenting on the break-up of the union between England and Ireland.

Can you identify where in the cartoon the artist has shown the following:
- the British Prime Minister, David Lloyd-George, preparing to end the union
- the province of Ulster about to be cut out of the Union
- the hopes that England and Ireland might one day be reunited?

> **Think**
>
> Look at picture A. Can you suggest any reasons why the union between England and Ireland might have broken down?

What were the key events in Ireland's relationship with England?

1169: The Normans arrive in Ireland. By 11/1 Henry II has claimed ownership of Ireland.

1541: Henry VIII declares himself King of Ireland.

1649: Oliver Cromwell's forces win the English Civil War and begin a military campaign to stamp out Catholic royalist support in Ireland.

1690: William of Orange defeats the forces of James II at the Battle of the Boyne, putting an end to hopes of a Catholic king in Ireland.

1798: The United Irishmen rebel against English rule. Demanding a united Ireland free from English rule, they are defeated at the Battle of Vinegar Hill.

1800: The Act of Union creates the United Kingdom of Great Britain and Ireland.

1845: The start of the Great Hunger (Potato Famine). 1.5 million die from disease and starvation.

1858: The Irish Republican Brotherhood (IRB) is formed in America by immigrants who had fled the famine. The IRB aims to overthrow English rule in Ireland by force.

1886: The first Home Rule Bill is drawn up by British Prime Minister Gladstone and Irish MP Parnell. It aims to give Ireland independence but is defeated by Protestant opposition in Ulster.

1907: The Sinn Fein political party is formed to campaign for complete freedom for Ireland.

1914: The outbreak of the First World War postpones further discussion of Home Rule. Many Irishmen fight for the British army in the hope that this will help persuade the government to give Home Rule to Ireland.

1916: Irish rebels seize key sites around Dublin and declare Ireland independent from England in the Easter Rising. The British army crush the rebellion. The leaders are executed and 3,000 rebels jailed.

1919: The Irish War of Independence is fought between the British army and the Irish Republican Army (IRA).

1921: The Anglo-Irish Treaty is signed. The six counties of Ulster (Northern Ireland) remain part of Britain, while the other counties become the Irish Free State. This is known as the partition of Ireland.

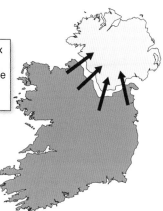

Activity

As you read the timeline, try to identify any events that you think might have damaged the relationship between England and Ireland. Make a list in your book.

What does the Doolough Tragedy tell us about the situation in Ireland in 1849?

As you have seen, by 1916 the relationship between England and Ireland had collapsed into bloodshed and would ultimately be broken up by the Anglo-Irish treaty in 1921. We may shed some light on why this happened by examining events in 1849 in a small part of the west of Ireland.

1 A group of hungry peasants are told to gather in the town of Louisburgh if they wished to receive food and poor relief (money to help them live).

2 Upon gathering in the town, the hungry crowds are told that the two Poor Law Guardians – Colonel Hosgrove and Captain Primrose – have left. They are told that if they want help, they will need to get themselves to Delphi, the hunting lodge of the Marquis of Sligo, for 7a.m. the next morning. This represented a journey of around sixteen miles across bleak hills and moors.

3 Hundreds of starving, poorly dressed families began the journey across the moors and hills to Delphi Lodge. The journey was made at night in driving rain and high winds. Many died along the way. The hardest part of the journey was across the mountains that surround the 'Black lake' that gives Doolough its name.

ATLANTIC OCEAN

The Doolough Pass looking south towards Delphi Lodge. The monument ➡ commemorates the hundreds of people who died in the Doolough Tragedy and all of those who died in the Great Hunger.

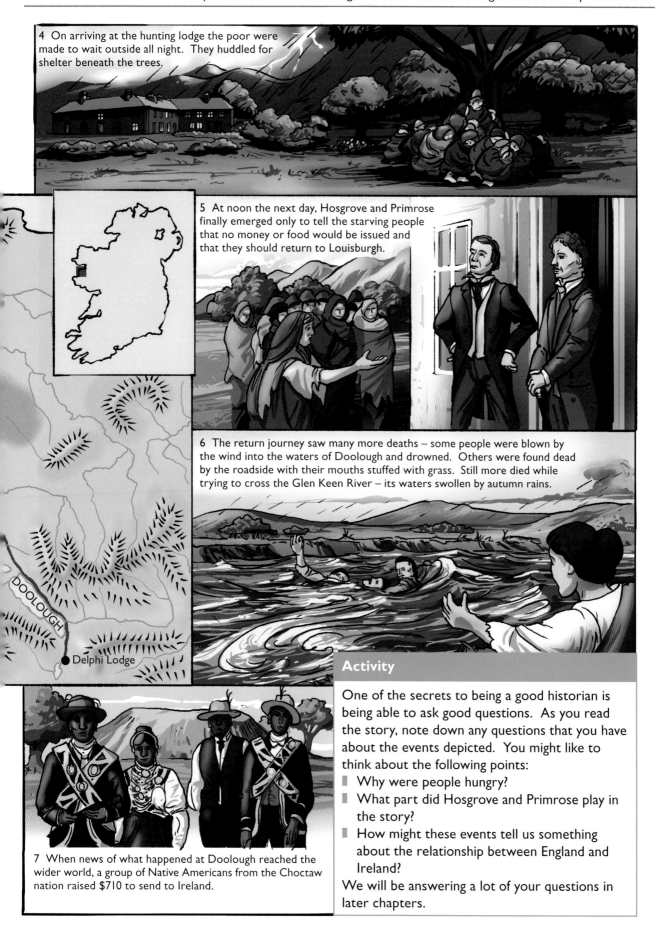

4 On arriving at the hunting lodge the poor were made to wait outside all night. They huddled for shelter beneath the trees.

5 At noon the next day, Hosgrove and Primrose finally emerged only to tell the starving people that no money or food would be issued and that they should return to Louisburgh.

6 The return journey saw many more deaths – some people were blown by the wind into the waters of Doolough and drowned. Others were found dead by the roadside with their mouths stuffed with grass. Still more died while trying to cross the Glen Keen River – its waters swollen by autumn rains.

DOOLOUGH

Delphi Lodge

7 When news of what happened at Doolough reached the wider world, a group of Native Americans from the Choctaw nation raised $710 to send to Ireland.

Activity

One of the secrets to being a good historian is being able to ask good questions. As you read the story, note down any questions that you have about the events depicted. You might like to think about the following points:

- Why were people hungry?
- What part did Hosgrove and Primrose play in the story?
- How might these events tell us something about the relationship between England and Ireland?

We will be answering a lot of your questions in later chapters.

6

How important was the Great Hunger in the breakdown of England's relationship with Ireland?

Who was to blame for the Great Hunger?

A

The Discovery of the Potato Blight by the artist Daniel MacDonald depicts the moment when an Irish family discover that their potato harvest has been ruined by a fungus or blight.

Can you find the following features in the painting:
- the ruined potatoes lying on the ground
- a bare-footed child
- the baby
- the girl who has collapsed in despair
- the discarded spade
- the woman peering at the ruined potatoes.

The people depicted in picture A are representative of the millions of poor farmers who, beginning in 1845, found that the potato crop upon which they relied for survival had been attacked by a fungus. Over the next seven years the crops would continue to fail.

These events are widely known as the Irish Potato Famine or the Great Hunger. Since the seventeenth century the poor people living in the west of Ireland had depended for survival on the potato crop. In many parts of the west, potatoes were all that would grow in the thin soil. In 1845 a fungus arrived in Ireland, probably brought by Clipper ships transporting passengers between Ireland and America.

Between 1845 and 1852 an estimated 1 million Irish people would die from lack of food; a further million would leave the country as emigrants seeking better lives abroad. As you saw in the previous chapter, for people like those in the town of Louisburgh, where the crop failure was total, death from starvation became a very real possibility.

Obviously, the failure of the potato crop represented a national tragedy for Ireland. However, the events of the 1840s in Ireland are still being argued over by historians today.

For example, historical writer Tim Pat Coogan has argued that the British government was in a large part responsible for the extent of the famine.

By contrast, other historians have argued that, while the British government might not have done enough, they did try to help but were handicapped by their beliefs that the government should interfere as little as possible in the running of the economy.

Activity

Imagine that you are going to help brief a talk show host who is going to be appearing on a show with two historians who are debating the role of the British government in the Great Hunger. How will you help her to feel prepared for the debate?

1 First, make a copy of the table below.

As you read the timeline of how the government attempted to deal with the famine on pages 64–65, add notes to your table. The first idea has been added for you.

Evidence to support the argument that the British government was in a large part responsible	Evidence to support the argument that the British government did try to help
In November 1845, Dublin citizens asked that the government stop exporting food out of Ireland and that public work schemes be set up to provide jobs. Their request was refused.	

2 Once you have completed your table, you will be ready to give advice to our talk show host. The questions below should help you to write your advice. Discuss them in pairs and then write your advice as a set of briefing notes.
   a) Whose side should she take? Do you think she should keep a neutral position (neither of the two sides)?
   b) Which pieces of evidence did the most to convince you of your conclusion?

How important was the Great Hunger in the breakdown of England's relationship with Ireland?

6

1845

- In November 1845 some Dublin citizens asked that the government ban the export of food out of Ireland and that public work schemes be set up to provide jobs. Their request was denied.
- In the same month the British Prime Minister, Sir Robert Peel, purchased £100,000 worth of maize from America. Due to weather conditions, however, this would not arrive in Ireland until early 1846.

⬆ Sir Robert Peel.

1846

- February 1846 saw the arrival of the first maize shipments from America. The Irish were unfamiliar with the milling, preparation and cooking of maize – this led to many cases of diarrhoea.
- The new British Prime Minister, Lord John Russell, made the decision to stop the importing of maize to Ireland. He said that importing food was hurting the profits of British landowners in Ireland and that the maize would be better used feeding British soldiers in India.
- Russell's government set up schemes to provide jobs for people in Ireland. They insisted that people must work for their food. In the minds of the government, to simply give people food would make them lazy. This meant that thousands of starving people were put to work on often pointless building schemes – digging holes and building roads that no one needed.

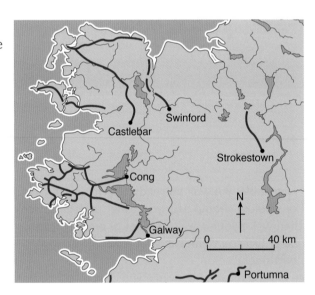

⬆ Map of so called 'famine roads' built in the west of Ireland.

1847

- In this year 4,000 ships left Irish ports carrying food. Many English landlords were mainly concerned with making a profit. To do this, they needed to export food to markets abroad. As food was being exported while millions went hungry, the army was often used to protect these food exports. In Westport, County Mayo, food was shipped under armed guard by British soldiers. In the same year, 400,000 Irish peasants starved.

⬆ The memorial to victims of the famine in Mayo.

- In January 1847 the public works projects were replaced by workhouses. Here, people could go for help in return for doing often back-breaking work. (You can read more about workhouses on page 130.) Workhouses were funded by local landlords, so to reduce the cost to themselves they began evicting their tenants. If tenants were forced off their land, they would no longer be the responsibility of the landlord. The Marquis of Sligo, for example, evicted 2,000 tenants in the village of Ballinrobe and turned the land over to cattle grazing. The tenants were faced with a choice of starvation, workhouse or emigration.

⬆ An engraving of a scene at an Irish workhouse during the famine.

1848

This year saw the blight once again wipe out the potato harvest. To make matters worse, due to deaths and emigration in previous years, fewer potatoes had actually been planted. However, the extension of the workhouse schemes does seem to have slowed the death rate from starvation.

1849

This was the year of the Doolough Tragedy (see pages 60–61). The British government began a scheme to try to persuade farmers to begin growing crops other than potatoes, such as green vegetables. The scheme was only partly successful as in many parts of the west, where the Irish farmers had been pushed onto the poorest land, potatoes remained the only crop that would grow.

Think

1. What has the story of the Great Hunger taught you about the relationship between Britain and Ireland?
2. Do you think that the British government did enough to help?
3. What events do you think might have done the most to create tension in the Anglo-Irish relationship?
4. Can you go back and answer any questions raised by the Doolough chapter (pages 60–61)?

6

How important was the Great Hunger in the breakdown of England's relationship with Ireland?

How important was the Great Hunger in the breakdown of Britain's relationship with Ireland?

You already know a lot about the events of the Great Hunger. The remainder of this section will help you to explore the other factors that damaged the relationship between Britain and Ireland.

From what you have read so far you could easily be left with the impression that the only cause of the breakdown of the relationship between Britain and Ireland was the reaction of the British government to the Great Hunger. The Great Hunger did indeed cause much resentment towards the government in London. Moreover, **emigrants** fleeing abroad to America and Australia carried with them stories of the callous nature of English rule. Indeed, it might be possible to suggest a direct link from the famine years to the rise of armed resistance to English rule by the **Fenians**. The mural below could be seen to make just such a connection.

A

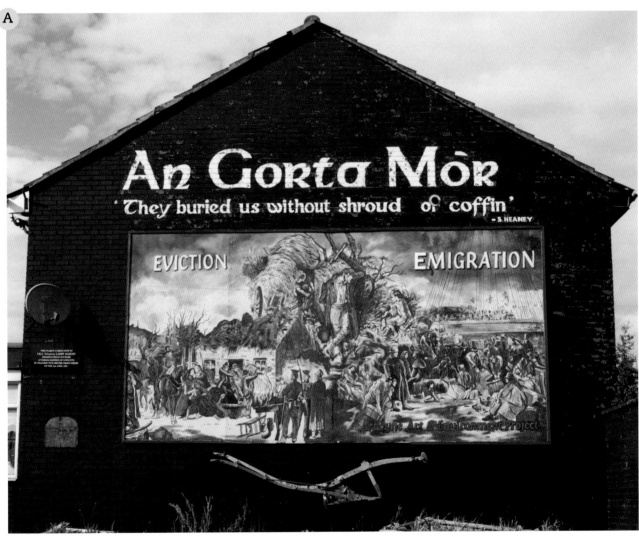

⬆ In this mural you can see an artist's reaction to the events of the period of the Great Hunger. In front of the mural you can see a plough – which was used as a symbol on the flags of the Irish Citizen Army during the 1916 rebellion in Dublin. It would appear that in this mural a connection is being made between the Great Hunger and the events of 1916.

The following text from an internet website for school students also makes a connection between the years of the Great Hunger and the rise of violent resistance to British rule in Ireland.

B

http://www.yourhistory.co.uk/great_famine

Your History - Great Famine

From the time of the Great Famine certain sections of the Irish population had lost faith in the British government. These people felt that the government neither listened to the complaints and grievances of the Irish nor did they care about such grievances.

This group rejected the idea that London had any right to impose rule on Ireland. Independence would have to be fought for – hence the armed uprising.

The events of the years of the Great Hunger were clearly horrific but it would be dangerous for us as historians to answer the question, 'How important was the Great Hunger in the breakdown of Britain's relationship with Ireland?' by only focusing on the famine. As historians we know that events usually have several, often inter-connected causes. In the remainder of this section we will consider how far the famine was the main cause of the breakdown in the Anglo-Irish relationship.

Three big issues lie at the heart of the strained relationship between Britain and Ireland. These are:

- **Religion**: Ireland was a predominantly Catholic country which was being ruled over by Protestant England.
- **Land**: The fight of the Irish peasants to control and own their own land was a key factor in their hatred of English landlords.
- **Home Rule**: Since its conquest by the Normans there existed a desire from some sectors of Irish society to gain Home Rule.

Many of these themes can be found in the street murals that have been painted over the years in parts of Northern Ireland. These works of art are themselves interpretations of Irish history but we can use them to see how artists have attempted to tell parts of the story of Irish history. Two of these murals are shown on page 68.

Activity

1 As you look at the murals think about what images have been used to show the three big issues of Irish history – 1) religion, 2) land, 3) Home Rule (see page 67). You might like to consider:
  - Why might British soldiers be featured?
  - Why might there be mention of the slaughter of Protestants and the desecration of churches? What theme of Irish history might this highlight?
  - Why might one mural wish the British soldiers a safe journey home?
2 Are there any of the three issues that the murals have not shown?

C

The English flag with the cross of St George (patron saint of England). The flag suggests that Ireland was, at least since Cromwell's time, controlled by England.

The phrase 'Lord Protector, Defender of the Protestant faith' showing the importance of the Protestant religion to some people in Ireland.

These are soldiers of Cromwell's New Model Army who went to Ireland to help put down anti-English rebels. Fighting between the two sides – English and Irish – would be a regular feature in Irish politics.

The phrase 'Catholicism is more than a religion it is a political power'– showing the importance of the Catholic religion to some people in Ireland.

⬆ A loyalist Belfast street mural showing Oliver Cromwell in Ireland. Cromwell had led English forces into Ireland in 1649 to crush Catholic support for King Charles I.

D

The green, white and orange colours of the Irish Republic flag. This is used by some people as the sign of Ireland ruling itself.

The Gaelic phrase *Slan Abhaile*, which means 'Safe Home'. This is a traditional Gaelic phrase used to wish people a safe journey home.

A sign saying 'England'.

British soldiers walking away. They are leaving Ireland.

⬅ A Catholic street mural in Derry / Londonderry looking forward and wishing for the departure of the British Army from Ireland.

Activity

3 At the end of this chapter, you are going to design a new street mural to be part of a display outside the National Museum in Dublin. Your mural needs to explain why, in your opinion, the relationship between England and Ireland had broken down by 1920.

Clearly, you might decide that you want to include information on the role of the famine. Consider these questions:

▌ What else, besides the Great Hunger, will you include?

▌ How much space will you give to the Great Hunger in your mural? Was it the main cause of the breakdown in the relationship?

The remainder of this section allows you to examine the other causes of the break in the relationship.

a) Make a copy of the table below:

Event	Summary of what happened and why it damaged the relationship	Score: Red, Amber, Green for the damage it did to the relationship	How might you represent this in your mural?
Catholic Emancipation			
Home Rule Campaign – part I			
The Young Ireland Movement			
The Land League			
Home Rule campaign – part 2			
Irish Republican Brotherhood			
The 1916 Easter Rising			
Sinn Fein			
War and Partition			

b) As you read the summary cards on pages 70–71 complete the summary chart. You will need to write a very short summary of each event and then decide how important it was in helping to damage the relationship with England. To help you do this you might consider:

▌ Was the event violent?

▌ Were lots of people involved?

▌ How did the English government react?

6

How important was the Great Hunger in the breakdown of England's relationship with Ireland?

Other causes of the breakdown in the Anglo-Irish relationship by 1920

1 Catholic Emancipation

Catholics made up the majority of the population of Ireland but were not given the same rights as Protestants. Catholics were not allowed to vote or stand as Members of Parliament. They were denied access to many top jobs. In the 1820s Daniel O'Connell launched a campaign which succeeded in winning Catholic Emancipation by 1829. Poor Catholics still complained bitterly at having to pay tithes to the Protestant Church and religion remained a source of tension in Ireland far into the twenty-first century. Many Catholics saw complete Irish Home Rule as the only solution.

1829

2 The Home Rule campaign – part 1

Encouraged by the success of Catholic Emancipation, Daniel O'Connell began to campaign against the Act of Union. His aim was for Home Rule, the creation of a Parliament in Dublin to make laws for Ireland (but with Queen Victoria remaining as monarch). O'Connell succeeded in getting tens of thousands of Irish people to support his idea and to attend 'Monster Meetings' – huge, peaceful rallies calling for Irish independence. In 1843 the government banned a Monster Meeting at Clontarf and arrested Daniel O'Connell. Some Irish people now began to argue that Home Rule could only be won by force.

3 The Young Ireland Movement

Inspired by revolutionary events in France, the Young Ireland Movement aimed for complete independence for Ireland. Independence would be won through violent revolution if necessary. The movement, which had both Catholic and Protestant members, launched a rebellion against British rule in 1848. The rebellion failed due to lack of support, lack of weapons and due to the fact that it coincided with the famine which had left many people too weak to fight. The British government punished three of the leaders with **transportation** to Australia.

4 The Land League

Much of the farming land in Ireland was owned by English landlords – many of whom did not live in Ireland. The Land League, formed in 1879 and led by Charles Stewart Parnell, fought to gain fair rent for Irish tenant farmers and ultimately to remove English landlords. From 1879 to 1882 a Land War was fought against landlords who tried to evict their tenants or raise their rents. The landlords were given support from the police, which often led to violence. Despite winning some victories with the Land Acts of 1881 and 1885 some within the Land League began to argue that the real solution to Ireland's land problem was Home Rule.

5 The Home Rule campaign – part 2

Parnell succeeded in persuading the British Prime Minister, Gladstone, to support the idea of Home Rule. Home Rule Bills were introduced into Parliament in 1886 and 1893. Both were defeated. A third Bill, passed in 1914, was put on hold by the outbreak of the First World War.

6 The Irish Republican Brotherhood

Formed in New York City in 1858 the Irish Republican Brotherhood (often referred to as the Fenians) aimed for total Irish freedom from English rule. Influenced by Irish migrants who had fled the Great Hunger, they plotted violence against England. This included bomb attacks on targets on the English mainland and efforts to free Fenian prisoners being held in English prisons.

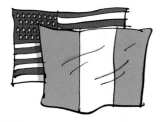

7 The 1916 Easter Rising

On 24 April 1916, rebels organised by the Irish Republican Brotherhood seized key sites around Dublin. They declared Ireland a Republic, completely independent from England. Over the following week, Britain deployed over 16,000 troops, artillery and a naval gunboat into the city to crush the rising, resulting in about 450 deaths and over 2,000 other casualties. The execution of the leaders of the Rising, along with the continued delay of Home Rule, rising casualties of the First World War and the threat of conscription, helped to strengthen the **radical nationalists**, Sinn Fein.

8 Sinn Fein

The **Sinn Fein** party, which had not taken part in the rebellion, gained support from veterans of the Rising as it pledged to fight for Home Rule and an Irish Parliament. Sinn Fein went on to win the general election in 1918, leading to their proclamation of an Irish Republic and the start of the Irish War of Independence.

9 War and partition

Beginning on 21 January 1919 in the Irish War of Independence, Irish republicans attempted to free Ireland from the United Kingdom. Meanwhile, Irish Unionists – who mostly lived in Ulster – were just as determined to maintain the Union. Seeking to calm the situation, the British government decided to divide Ireland into Northern and Southern Ireland. The Government of Ireland Act 1920 entered into force on 3 May 1921 and provided that Northern Ireland would consist of the six counties, while the remainder of the island would form Southern Ireland.

Activity

4 Once you have completed your table from Activity 3 (page 69), you are ready to design your Irish street mural. Keep in mind the big question of this section:

How important was the Great Hunger in the breakdown of England's relationship with Ireland?

Remember, murals are interpretations of history and in Ireland they are often one-sided, favouring either the Irish or pro-English view of events. What will your mural do? Will you present events from an Irish or an English point of view? Or, will you remember your training as a historian and try to show both sides of the story?

You will also need to think about what images you will include. How will you show the importance of religion, land or the desire of the Irish people for independence?

Don't forget that you can go back to the timeline on pages 64–65 and use events from this in your mural.

The Big Picture of the British Empire, 1500–1900

You may remember having read about the **Mughal Empire** in *Making Sense of History 1509–1745*. The British Empire was much larger, and at its height controlled one-quarter of the world's population.

A

In this section you will consider the effect the British Empire had on the people who lived in it and judge whether it was something to be proud of. We start by looking at the three stages of Empire, from its beginning to its height.

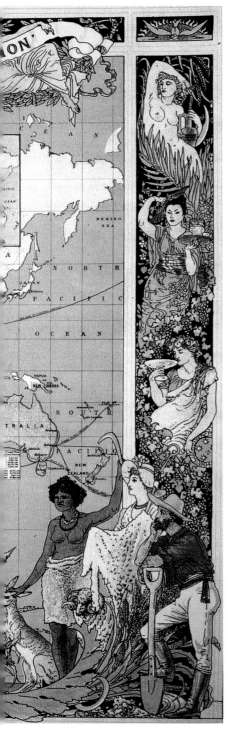

Stage 1: The beginnings of the empire

At first, it was the Spanish and the Portuguese who led the way exploring the world's oceans, establishing colonies and making money from it. During the sixteenth century, Spain became exceedingly wealthy from mining silver in South America. Spanish **galleons** soon became a target for English pirates like Sir Francis Drake who, encouraged by Queen Elizabeth (1558–1603), relieved them of their treasure. Then, in 1585, England attempted to found its own colony at Roanoke on the east coast of North America. The colony failed, but by 1607 the English had established a permanent colony further up the coast at Jamestown.

Sometimes, European settlers came into conflict with the Native Americans but even when relations were friendly, death was often not far behind. The locals had little resistance to the European diseases the colonists took with them and thousands died as a result.

Think

Look carefully at the imagery around the outside of map A. Britannia sits on the globe, suggesting that Britain was the world's leading power. What other messages do you think the images give about the British Empire?

⬅ A map of the world published in 1886. The lands shaded pink were part of the British Empire at that time.

⬆ An English painting of a Native American in 1585.

The Big Picture

Stage 2: Empire in the seventeenth and eighteenth centuries

By the 1620s, English colonists had established sugar and tobacco plantations in the West Indies. They relied on the labour of African slaves who were transported across the Atlantic (see pages 20–21). The trade in slaves, tobacco and sugar generated huge profits and created wealth in the English ports of Bristol and Liverpool.

British merchants were also making profits as far away as India. After setting up a number of trading posts, the **East India Company** gradually took more and more control over Indian territory. After driving out the French in 1757, the British were the dominant power in India.

By the end of the eighteenth century, Britain had established a foothold even further away in Australia. Many of the first British colonists were convicts who had been transported there as a punishment.

Think

Looking at picture C, why do you think some Aboriginal people turned to drinking alcohol after British settlers arrived?

C

⬆ Aborigines on the edge of Sydney, from a painting made in 1830. Aborigines – native Australians – were forced off the land by the British government and their traditional way of life was destroyed.

Stage 3: World empire in the nineteenth century

As a result of the Industrial Revolution (see pages 16–19), Britain was by far the richest and most powerful country in the world and its empire continued to grow. Britain used its navy to defend the trade routes running between its different colonies and to move soldiers and supplies around its empire. The size and strength of the British navy allowed it to impose its will, even on countries, like China, that were not officially part of the empire (see pages 82–83).

By the end of the century, Africa had been divided up between the European powers so quickly that historians have described this as the Scramble for Africa. British farmers and miners were able to settle in some of the richest areas, often coming into conflict with native populations who were usually no match for the superior military technology of the British.

The British claimed, that by preaching Christianity and imposing their own laws and customs, they were spreading civilisation. In some parts of the empire, schools, hospitals and railways were built which helped reinforce the idea that the empire was a force for good; something the British people should be proud of.

Activity

Look back over the three stages in the development of the British Empire on pages 73–75.
1 Make a list of all the ways the British Empire had a positive impact.
2 Make a list of the ways the British Empire may have had a negative impact.
3 In pairs or small groups, compare your two lists and discuss what you notice. Is there a pattern?

Think

How are the forces of civilisation and barbarism shown differently in picture D? What does this reveal about British attitudes?

D

⬆ *From the Cape to Cairo*, 1902. Britannia (Britain) leads soldiers and colonists against Africans as Civilisation conquers Barbarism.

Would Cecil Rhodes have wanted a statue of Julius Caesar in his office?

Cecil Rhodes was one of the people who, in the nineteenth century, argued most strongly that Britain should control as much of Africa as possible. He was one of the brains behind what some historians call the Scramble for Africa. He firmly believed that Africa, Britain and the world in general would benefit from the growth of the British Empire.

Back in 55 BC the Romans had some strong ideas about their empire. In this Stepped Enquiry you will have an opportunity to compare the motivation behind the Roman and the British Empires. Was empire building driven by selfish motives or by a desire to help other people around the world?

In doing this you will also work towards deciding if the British should be proud of the British Empire.

A

A cartoon of 1892 showing the British-born politician, Cecil Rhodes. His right foot is standing on South Africa, his left foot is standing in Egypt. Can you find the following:
• the continent of Africa
• the rifle
• an adventurer's pith helmet
• a telegraph wire?

Think

What is the cartoonist saying about Cecil Rhodes in picture A?

7

Should the British Empire be a source of national pride?

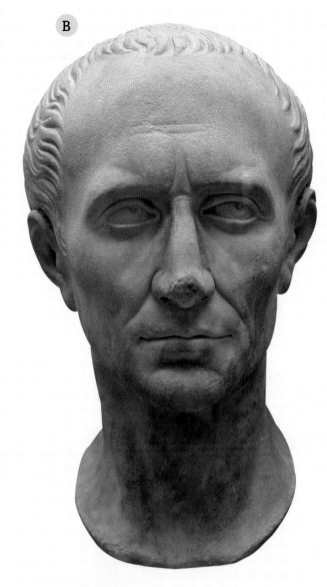

B

⬆ A bust of the Roman leader Julius Caesar. In 55 BC, Caesar led a Roman army to invade Britain. On this occasion he was unsuccessful, defeated partly by bad weather which wrecked his ships. However, he returned with a larger army in 54 BC, fought several battles and returned to Rome with several important hostages. Britain finally became a part of the Roman Empire in AD 43.

Enquiry Step 1: First evidence – asking questions

Historians often like to work out why things happen. They try to explain the causes of things and they try to look for similarities between causes to see if they can learn lessons about the past. In this enquiry, therefore, we are going to try to answer a rather strange question:

Would Cecil Rhodes have wanted a statue of Julius Caesar in his office?

As we have no real way of knowing how Cecil Rhodes felt about collecting Roman statues we will need to consider a couple of important questions.

1 Why did Cecil Rhodes want to expand the British Empire in Africa? When we examine the motives of key individuals from the past, their motives can provide insights into why things happened.

2 Did Julius Caesar have similar reasons for wanting to add Britain to the Roman Empire?

If we are going to answer this enquiry question we need to start by first working out why Cecil Rhodes wanted to expand the British Empire. Here is one reason why Rhodes thought that the growth of the empire was a good idea:

'We are the first race of the world and the more of the world we inhabit the better it is for the human race.'

Rhodes believed that Britain was the greatest civilisation on Earth and that it was Britain's destiny to conquer other countries and spread this civilisation around the world.

Write this idea in your own words onto a piece of card. Then read through the cartoon strip on pages 78–79 telling the story of Cecil Rhodes and his ideas about empire, and try to make more cause cards.

Rhodes' ideas about the expansion of the British Empire

1 Rhodes arrived in South Africa in 1870. He went initially to see if the climate would improve his health. After some work in farming he turned to, and made a considerable personal fortune from, diamond mining. It was common practice for the British to make use of the local black population as a workforce in the diamond mines. Rhodes' mines were no exception. Making a fortune confirmed for him the idea that if Britain could take over new lands they could easily obtain raw materials and make money for Britain.

2 In 1880 Rhodes entered politics in South Africa and within ten years had become Prime Minister of the Cape Colony. Many of the laws passed by Rhodes' government were designed to benefit British settlers. For example, the Glen Grey Act sought to push black farmers off their land so it could be used for industry.

3 Britain, as part of the scramble for Africa, was engaged in a competition with other European countries to try to control its best land. The greater a country's empire the more political power it would be seen to have. Rhodes believed that Britain needed to expand territorially in Africa – leading him to support the 1895 Jameson Raid which tried to take control of the Boer-controlled Transvaal. Rhodes wanted to bring as much of the world's land as possible under British rule. The more land the British ruled in Africa, the less its potential enemies (Germans, Portuguese or Boers) would be able to take.

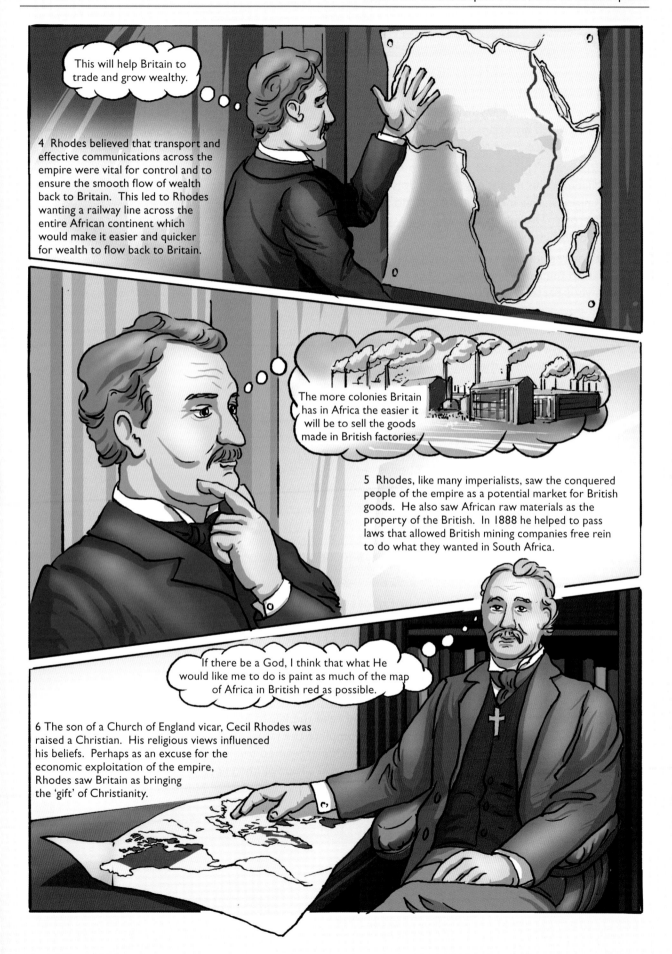

This will help Britain to trade and grow wealthy.

4 Rhodes believed that transport and effective communications across the empire were vital for control and to ensure the smooth flow of wealth back to Britain. This led to Rhodes wanting a railway line across the entire African continent which would make it easier and quicker for wealth to flow back to Britain.

The more colonies Britain has in Africa the easier it will be to sell the goods made in British factories.

5 Rhodes, like many imperialists, saw the conquered people of the empire as a potential market for British goods. He also saw African raw materials as the property of the British. In 1888 he helped to pass laws that allowed British mining companies free rein to do what they wanted in South Africa.

If there be a God, I think that what He would like me to do is paint as much of the map of Africa in British red as possible.

6 The son of a Church of England vicar, Cecil Rhodes was raised a Christian. His religious views influenced his beliefs. Perhaps as an excuse for the economic exploitation of the empire, Rhodes saw Britain as bringing the 'gift' of Christianity.

Enquiry Step 2: Suggesting an answer

You should now have a set of cards summarising the reasons why Cecil Rhodes wanted to expand the British Empire. Can you group any of the cards together?

Do any of the cards have anything in common?
One way in which historians sort out why things happen is to categorise them into types. We are going to use four categories:

a Economic: This means anything to do with money, jobs or resources.
b Military: This means anything to do with wars, the army and fighting.
c Religious: This means anything to do with Gods and belief.
d Personal: This means anything to do with Cecil Rhodes himself.

1 Sort your set of cards under the headings above. What do the card sets tell you? Discuss this with your partner. Which is the biggest pile? What does that tell you about the driving forces behind the building of the British Empire?

2 Now arrange the cards onto a large piece of paper as shown in the diagram.
a What connections can you make? Draw lines between cards that are connected and along the lines explain why.
b Do any of the causes have more connections than others? What does this tell you about the reasons why Rhodes wanted to expand the British Empire?

3 Write a short explanation of why Cecil Rhodes thought expanding the British Empire was a good idea.

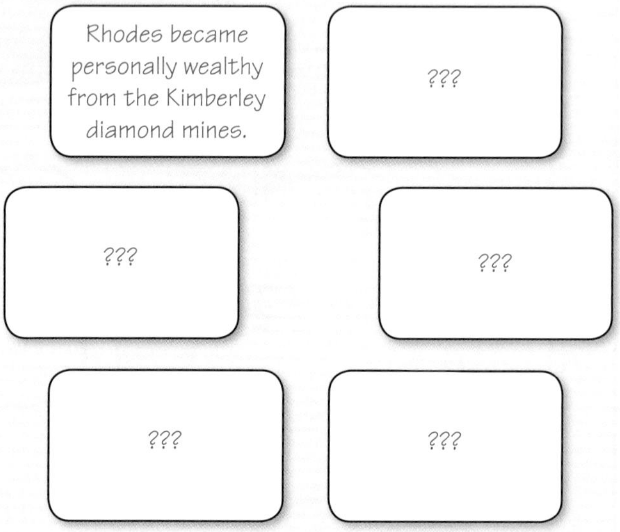

> Rhodes became personally wealthy from the Kimberley diamond mines.

> ???

> ???

> ???

> ???

> ???

Enquiry Step 3: Developing your answer

Now that we have a good idea about why Rhodes wanted to build an empire we need to return to our enquiry question:

Would Cecil Rhodes have wanted a statue of Julius Caesar in his office?

What we are looking to do is see if there were any similarities between what motivated the two empire builders, Caesar and Rhodes.

Copy the table below into your notebook. As you read the information about Julius Caesar and Britain you will need to complete the table. In the left-hand column note down all of the reasons why Rhodes wanted to expand the empire. The first one has been partly done for you. You will then need to decide if Caesar had similar ideas.

Reasons for Rhodes wanting to expand the British Empire	Similar ideas to Caesar?	What proof did you find?
The British were a superior civilisation and it was their destiny to conquer other countries.	Yes	

1 The island is thickly populated, and much tin is also carried from the British Isles to Gaul*.

4 Britain has gold and silver and other metals. The ocean, too, produces pearls.

2 We will be able to take important hostages back to Rome and demand that the tribes pay a large sum of money to Rome every year as tribute**.

5 There are an infinite number of men, very many buildings and very large herds. They (the Britons) use either bronze or gold money. There is timber of every kind.

3 The Britons are sending help to Rome's enemies in Gaul. If we conquer the Britons then we would be able to stop them helping our enemies.

6 No other Roman leader has ever succeeded in conquering Britain. A victory there would make me famous.

⬆ Julius Caesar's possible reasons for wanting to conquer Britain.
*Gaul is modern-day France, and an area the Romans were trying to add to their empire before they looked to Britain.
**Tribute was a type of tax paid to the Roman Emperor by countries that had been conquered.

Step 4: Concluding your enquiry

You have now done a lot of thinking about the reasons why both Julius Caesar and Cecil Rhodes might have wanted to build an empire. Have a look at your completed table, then discuss as a whole class:

1 What does the completed table tell you?
2 What are the key similarities between Julius Caesar, and Cecil Rhodes' motives for wanting to build an empire? Are there any differences between their motives?
3 Would Cecil Rhodes have wanted a statue of Julius Caesar in his office? Write a short statement in your book. Remember to use connectives such as 'because' to help you explain your reasoning.
4 Now you know WHY the British wanted to expand their empire, does it make you feel proud, or ashamed, of the empire? Add your ideas to the lists of positives and negatives you began on page 75.

What have the British ever done for us?

In the last Stepped Enquiry you studied why the British built an empire in the nineteenth century. In this chapter you will look more directly at whether the empire benefited the people the British conquered.

In 1839 a guide book published for the London and Birmingham Grand Junction Railway contained the following boast:

> *It is a proud feeling to an Englishman to know that the products of the thousand busy hands and whirling wheels around him are destined to increase the comfort, refinement or splendour of nations spread far and wide over the globe.*

⬇The British Empire in 1900.

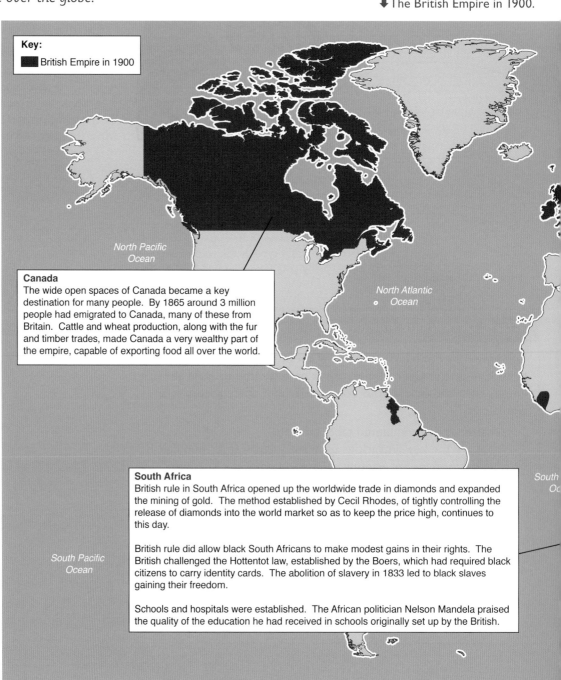

Key:
British Empire in 1900

North Pacific Ocean

Canada
The wide open spaces of Canada became a key destination for many people. By 1865 around 3 million people had emigrated to Canada, many of these from Britain. Cattle and wheat production, along with the fur and timber trades, made Canada a very wealthy part of the empire, capable of exporting food all over the world.

North Atlantic Ocean

South Pacific Ocean

South Oc

South Africa
British rule in South Africa opened up the worldwide trade in diamonds and expanded the mining of gold. The method established by Cecil Rhodes, of tightly controlling the release of diamonds into the world market so as to keep the price high, continues to this day.

British rule did allow black South Africans to make modest gains in their rights. The British challenged the Hottentot law, established by the Boers, which had required black citizens to carry identity cards. The abolition of slavery in 1833 led to black slaves gaining their freedom.

Schools and hospitals were established. The African politician Nelson Mandela praised the quality of the education he had received in schools originally set up by the British.

The products of Britain's mills and factories, it was argued, were going to improve the lives of people throughout the British Empire. On these pages we will examine whether there was any truth in this claim.

Activity

As you read about the achievements of the British Empire on pages 82–83 select the three things that you think British people could feel most proud about. Add your ideas to the list of positives you began on page 75.

India
India was regarded as the jewel of the empire. Under British rule, trade from India increased from 2% of national income to 20% by 1900. From 1891 onwards the British invested in improving irrigation, doubling the amount of farm land. The British rulers also created a postal system, opened universities and hospitals, improved river travel and built 40,000 miles of railways. British rule could also be seen to have had a beneficial impact in removing some of the more unpleasant aspects of local culture. British missionaries worked with local leaders to put an end to *suti*, the custom of forcing widows to commit suicide following the deaths of their husbands. Cricket, that most English of sports, also found a fertile home on Indian soil.

Hong Kong
The island of Hong Kong was added to the British Empire by the Treaty of Nanjing in 1842 (see page 85). Under British rule, Hong Kong became an economic powerhouse in South East Asia. From simple beginnings where the British promoted the setting up of coffee farms, 1856 also saw the setting up of HSBC (The Hong Kong and Shanghai Bank of Commerce) which today employs nearly 70,000 people.

Hong Kong gave many Chinese refugees an escape route from instability and war in mainland China, and provided a safe haven for people fleeing the Taiping Rebellion, a vast civil war in southern China that killed around 20 million people. As elsewhere in the empire, the British set up schools and a university.

Ceylon (Now Sri Lanka)
Ceylon was unified under British rule after 1815. The British increased the amount of land under cultivation from 460,000 to 3.2 million acres. A total of 2,300 miles of roads and 2,900 miles of railroads were built, improving transport and communication across the island nation. Before the British arrived, there were no hospitals, but under British rule the number rose to 65 while the number of schools rose from 170 to 2,900.

Pacific Ocean

Indian Ocean

Australia and New Zealand
British rule in Australia started using the continent as a penal colony, a dumping ground for criminals. Many of these were transported for petty crimes such as stealing a loaf of bread. However, once those transported to Australia had finished their prison sentences, they could apply for grants of land. This often meant that ex-convicts ended up better off in Australia than in Britain. By 1900, improvements in refrigeration meant that meat from the farms of Australia and New Zealand could be exported all over the world. British rule in Australia introduced parliamentary democracy, just as it had in India, Canada and other parts of the empire. Australia and New Zealand became a home for British sports such as rugby and cricket with both of these countries continuing to produce many world-class athletes.

Tea, death and drugs: What is wrong with Betts' board game?

In this chapter, you will study the war which broke out between Britain and China in 1840–41. As this war with China happened as part of the expansion of the British Empire you will also gather information to help you decide if the British were right to be proud of their empire.

In 1853 a publishing company in London produced a board game. In this game players were able to take a tour of the British Empire and in doing so would learn something about the places and people who lived in the 'Empire where the sun never set'. If a player happened to land upon the square for the British colony of Hong Kong they would be able to read the following description:

> *Hong Kong is a small island on the south coast of China, near to Canton. It was taken possession of by the British in the war with China in 1841, and a settlement was formed on it in the ensuing year. The situation of this island, and our relations with China, have given to the settlement great importance.*

If a Chinese person had played the board game in 1853, they might have had a very different opinion about the war of 1840 and how the British got hold of Hong Kong.

A board game of the ➡
British Empire made
in 1853.

Activity

As you read the story of the Opium Wars consider the following questions.
1 What is wrong with the entry for Hong Kong on the 1853 board game? What does it miss out? As you read the text note down any new information that you learn that wasn't included on the board game.
2 How would you write a more factually balanced entry? What new information would you include? Try to keep your entry to around 50–60 words.
3 Add ideas to your lists of positives and negatives you began on page 75.

A remarkable journey

In September 1792 three ships packed with British made goods and led by Lord McCartney, a British diplomat who had successfully led British missions to Russia, set sail for China. Some 390 million people lived in China – all of whom could become customers for British traders. Lord McCartney's mission was to persuade the Chinese Emperor Qian Long to allow this trade to happen.

After ten months at sea McCartney and his men arrived in China and were granted a meeting with the Emperor. The Chinese Emperor did not want to do business with the British and flatly refused to trade.

The British were very disappointed. They wanted to sell their products to the millions of Chinese people and they were desperate for Chinese goods – particularly tea. Tea was needed to refresh the British workers and stop them from drinking alcohol.

Tea for opium

In order to get their hands on tea the British came up with the following scheme:

1   From 1800 they started loading their ships with opium in British-controlled India. (Opium is a highly addictive drug made from the seeds of poppies. It ruins the health of those who use it.)
2   The ships then sailed on to China and illegally traded the opium. Opium had been banned in China since the 1720s, so the British bribed Chinese officials and opium continued to flood into China. They used the money from this to buy tea and other goods.
3   Many Chinese people became addicted to opium. In some areas, one in every ten Chinese people became addicted to the drug. This addiction guaranteed future customers for these British 'drug dealers'.
4   The Emperor became increasingly angry but British traders didn't care. They were getting the goods they wanted – and were making lots of money.

The Emperor strikes back

Opium ruined the health of many Chinese people. An estimated 10 million Chinese people became addicted. The Emperor's own son died of an opium overdose.

⬆ A front cover of *The British Empire* magazine. In it you can see a figure representing Britain feeding opium to a Chinese man.

In March 1839 a new man, Lin Tse Hsu, was given the job of preventing more opium reaching China. He ordered all European and British traders to hand over their opium. When they refused, he sealed off Canton where the foreign merchants lived. He ordered Chinese warships to block the river and cut off the trade. Eventually the British gave in and handed over 20,283 boxes of opium. All the opium was burnt! Lin then expelled the British merchants and ruled that any British ship carrying opium in Chinese waters would be captured and its officers executed.

Gunboats

The British merchants demanded that their government take action. They wanted compensation for their losses and the opium trade restored. British Prime Minister Lord Palmerston agreed. He declared war on China in 1840 and sent warships to launch an attack.

The modern British ships and weapons were too much for the Chinese. After two years, the British won. In the peace treaty that followed, the Chinese had to agree to continue the opium trade, open up more of China for British traders and give Britain the small island of Hong Kong for the next 170 years.

How far do lard-coated cartridges explain the Indian Mutiny of 1857?

In this chapter, as part of your investigation into whether the empire benefited the people the British conquered, you will consider the impact of British rule in India.

The **East India Company** was a business established in 1600 in order to make a profit from trade with India. Within 150 years, the Company was making a massive fortune and ruled over large parts of India. It even had its own army, which relied heavily on the service of Indian soldiers called **sepoys**.

In May 1857, sepoys stationed in the town of Meerut rose up against their British officers. The revolt began after some of the men were jailed for refusing to use the new gunpowder cartridges they had been provided with. There were rumours that the cartridges had been coated with animal fat from pigs and cows, to keep them waterproof. As the ends had to be bitten off before use, this presented a problem for Muslim and Hindu troops. Muslims regard pigs as unclean and Hindus believe cows to be sacred.

On 9 May, the sepoys broke into the jail and released the prisoners, before massacring the British officers and their families.

For the Victorians, the cause of the mutiny was simple – it was down to the superstitious and ignorant religious beliefs of the sepoys, who were inferior to good British Christians! However, the revolt spread quickly, attracting peasants, local landlords and even some of the Indian nobility. Clearly, there was much unhappiness at British rule.

It took the British more than a year to put down the mutiny. During that time both sides committed terrible atrocities. British troops often went in search of revenge. For example, when they recaptured the town of Cawnpore, they arrested suspected rebels and made them lick up the blood of British victims before executing them. Perhaps most shocking was the punishment carried out in the town of Peshawar, where forty rebels were strapped to the barrels of cannon and blown apart.

> **Think**
>
> How does the artist make the British seem heroic compared with the Indian tiger in picture A? Why?

A

◀ A cartoon from the British magazine *Punch*. It shows the British lion attacking a tiger (representing the Indian mutineers).

Causes of the mutiny

1
At first, officers of the East India Company had mixed with sepoys, learning the language and even taking Indian wives. By 1857 even junior officers stayed away from sepoys, treating them as inferiors.

2
Areas under British control were heavily taxed. The company became much richer, but many landowning Indian families went into debt and were forced to borrow from moneylenders.

3
After 1848, the British introduced a law giving them the power to seize Indian land if the ruler died without an heir.

4
The British also took land away if they felt the Indian rulers were not doing a good enough job.

5
There were no promotion prospects for sepoys. Indian troops could give years of faithful service and still not be made officers, while younger British soldiers were frequently given command.

6
The number of Christian missionaries in India was increasing. Some British officers preached to their sepoys and in one regiment Bibles were translated and handed to the troops.

7
In 1856, the company ended the sepoys' pensions and cut rates of pay.

8
Previously, sepoys had received bonus pay for fighting abroad; now, all new recruits had to fight wherever they were sent and the bonuses were scrapped.

⬆ A nineteenth-century Indian painting of Rani Lakshmi. Rani Lakshmi was an Indian princess who died in battle against the British. Rani was angry when the British seized her husband's land after he died.

The British realised that things would have to change in India. After 1858, the East India Company was abolished and India was ruled directly by the British Parliament. This was the start of the period known as the 'British **Raj**' that lasted from 1858 to 1947. The number of British soldiers in India was massively increased to prevent any future rebellion. Law and order was restored but the relationship between Britain and India would never be the same again.

Activity

1 Make a copy of the Venn diagram. We have labelled one circle but labelling the other two is your task. Looking at the numbered list of causes of mutiny on this page, which other headings could you classify the reasons under?

2 Add the numbers from your list of causes to the correct parts of your Venn diagram.

3 What does your completed Venn diagram reveal about the causes of the Indian Mutiny? Was it simply a question of lard-coated cartridges or is there more to it than that?

4 What has this case study revealed about British rule? Did everyone benefit from the empire? Discuss this in pairs or small groups and add ideas to your lists of positives and negatives you began on page 75.

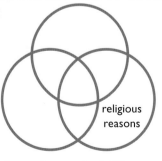

religious reasons

Should the British Empire be a source of national pride?

Now it is time to sum up your learning from this section and form a judgement about whether the British were right to be proud of their empire.

In 2014, as we were writing this book, YouGov.co.uk ran a poll asking people their views on the British Empire. The results showed, 'that by three to one, British people think the British Empire is something to be proud of rather than ashamed of – they also tend to think it left its colonies better off, and a third would like it to still exist.'

Yet this is a question that has long divided historians and continues to do so today. In this chapter you will be encouraged to make up your own mind and to understand why it is so difficult for historians to agree about the British Empire.

Victorian pride

For the Victorians it was simple – the empire was a force for good. School children were taught to feel proud of the empire while writers like Kipling persuaded adult readers that the British had a duty to help the 'lesser breeds' they encountered. At the heart of these attitudes was a belief that the British were a superior race who would bring civilisation and progress to the people they ruled over.

> **Think**
>
> Discuss with a partner any other messages that the plate in picture A gives about the British Empire. For example, what might the central figures symbolise?

A

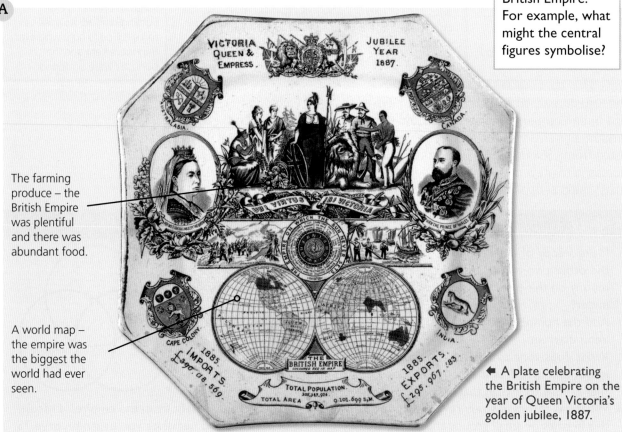

The farming produce – the British Empire was plentiful and there was abundant food.

A world map – the empire was the biggest the world had ever seen.

← A plate celebrating the British Empire on the year of Queen Victoria's golden jubilee, 1887.

Debates among historians

The impact of the British Empire has created much debate and controversy among historians. Below are quotes from two historians with dramatically opposing views.

B

The historian Niall Ferguson, 2003

'… no organisation in history has done more to promote the free movement of goods, capital and labour than the British Empire in the nineteenth and early twentieth centuries. And no organisation has done more to impose Western norms of law, order and governance around the world. For much (though certainly not all) of its history, the British Empire acted as an agency for relatively incorrupt government … there therefore seems a plausible case that empire enhanced global welfare – in other words, it was a Good Thing.'

C

The historian Richard Gott, 2011

'The creation of the British Empire caused large portions of the global map to be tinted a rich vermilion [red], and the colour turned out to be peculiarly appropriate. Britain's empire was established, and maintained for more than two centuries, through bloodshed, violence, brutality, conquest and war. Not a year went by without large numbers of its inhabitants being obliged to suffer for their involuntary participation in the colonial experience. Slavery, famine, prison, battle, murder, extermination – these were their various fates.'

Activity

1 Read the views of Niall Ferguson and Richard Gott above. Write a short summary of their views.
2 Draw a copy of the spectrum below and put your summaries from Activity 1 under the labels 'Ferguson' and 'Gott'.

Ferguson   **Gott**

3 Study each of the experiences of the Empire characters on pages 90–91. Decide where you would place them on your copy of the spectrum based on their testimony. Be prepared to explain your decisions.
4 Use this to add information to the lists of 'positives' and 'negatives' you began on page 75.

Imperial characters

A Zulu warrior in 1880

In 1879, the British invaded our lands. Despite our bravery, our spears were no match for British rifles. Now, just a year later, the Zulu kingdom has been split up and the British are in control.

An Indian school boy in 1900

I'm happy about the century I scored in cricket today! My friends at school gave me three cheers and my British teachers applauded my efforts. My father, who serves in the British Army, will be pleased when I write to him. Nowadays, the British make sure that the children of Indian soldiers are given good education in schools.

An Australian Aborigine in 1830

Our people have lived here for thousands of years, living off the land around us. Then the white settlers turned up with their fences and their cattle. We're treated as savages because we prefer to wander rather than settle in houses. The British think they own the land and now our way of life is all but gone.

A poor Indian farmer in 1876

Out in the countryside, life is much harder. This year, 1876, has seen a terrible drought that has caused our harvests to fail. There is still enough food saved from previous harvests but the British have sent this surplus grain back to England to keep down the cost of food for their own people. Meanwhile, we starve.

Why historians argue

It is clear that different people living in the empire had different lives to one another. In other words, there was a **diversity** of people's experiences.

Historians must consider factors such as when a person lived, whether they lived in the countryside or the town, which part of the world they lived in and whether they were rich or poor. All of these things could have had a big effect on that person's experience of the British Empire.

Historians sometimes select evidence from the past to support their own point of view. They may focus on certain types of people and this can affect how they interpret the British Empire.

The Oba (King) of Benin in 1897

In 1897, the British invaded my land after I refused to trade with them. They removed me from power and destroyed the royal palace, stealing our most sacred religious objects in the process. They slaughtered hundreds of my warriors and sent me into exile.

A Victorian missionary in 1898

The empire has spread Christianity and British rule of law, ending many cruel and barbaric customs. For example, before the British took control of the African kingdom of Benin, the rulers practised human sacrifice! We soon put a stop to that ghastly business!

A Canadian settler in 1870

I'm one of the many British settlers in Canada. What a Great land this is! The trees I cut down provide timber for export all over the world. We also grow wheat and other crops, which are traded on the world's markets and have made Canada wealthy. We, like the white settlers in Australia, New Zealand and South Africa, are self-governing. This means we have the freedom to make more of our own political decisions.

Activity

It seems unlikely that historians will ever agree about whether we should feel proud of the British Empire, so you are going to make up your own mind! You are going to design your own version of the plate you saw on page 88.

1 In pairs or small groups, discuss the lists of positives and negatives you have been building throughout this section. Was the British Empire something to be proud of, a source of shame, or a mixture of the two?

2 Choose from your lists the ten pieces of information which you think best sum up the British Empire. Use all of the information in this section (pages 72–89) to help you. Compare your choices with other students – be prepared to disagree!

3 Once you have decided what you want to include in your design, think about how you will show this on the plate. What illustrations will you use? Make a rough plan in your exercise book.

4 Draw your final design on a paper plate and write a brief paragraph explaining what messages it gives about the British Empire.

Think

Do you think that Ferguson and Gott (see page 89) looked at the same kind of evidence about the same kind of people?

How significant was the French Revolution?

By now you may have looked at the significance of the Norman Conquest and of the execution of Charles I. This section looks at the significance of the French Revolution.

As you may remember 'significance' is ultimately a judgement – an opinion. Different historians will have different views. That judgement will probably be based on four criteria:

Immediate impact
The initial change and the way people reacted to this at the time.

Short-term effects
The amount of change in the next few years; the bigger and wider the effect, the greater the significance.

Medium-term effects
The amount of change in the following decades; the bigger and wider the effect, the greater the significance.

Long-term effects
Lasting effects: the most significant historical events will be ones that still affect our lives today.

What was the French Revolution?

Louis XVI had become King of France in 1774 and had not ruled his country well. By 1789, France was near **bankruptcy** having taken part in two wars which it could not afford. There was not enough money coming in from taxes as the clergy (the First Estate) and the nobles (the Second Estate) who had most of the wealth were exempt from paying them. Instead, the lower and middle classes (the Third Estate) – who had far less wealth – were heavily taxed. This tax inequality resulted in great anger from the lower classes – an anger which grew as this group had no political voice at all.

In 1789 France was an **absolute monarchy** which meant Louis could rule without consulting an elected body. However, faced with bankruptcy he was forced to call a meeting of the **Estates General**, a body which contained representatives of all three estates and was only summoned in times of crisis. From the start it was obvious that Louis did not want to give the Third Estate as much power as the other two. Members of the Third Estate were appalled and had had enough. They set up their own democratic government, the National Assembly, and were soon joined by the majority of the members of the other two estates.

On 14 July 1789 the people of Paris hit the streets in support and stormed the Bastille prison in Paris, releasing its inmates and gunpowder stores. The next morning the King, Louis XVI, asked one of his advisers whether this was a revolt. He replied, 'No sire, it is a revolution'.

A

⬆ A contemporary cartoon showing a peasant being crushed by the weight of taxes while a noble and a clergyman stand on top.

Think

1 What is picture A saying about the situation in France in 1789?
2 If you had been in the Third Estate (the man under the rock) what would your reaction to the revolution have been?

The adviser was correct. In a matter of weeks a democratic government had been established; the French Revolution had begun.

Now we know what the French Revolution was, we can begin to look at how significant it was. In the picture below you can see an artist's impression of people's immediate reaction to the revolution at one of the first meetings of the National Assembly in 1789. Louis had locked them out of their normal meeting room so they met in the king's indoor tennis court instead, and took an oath never to stop meeting until the government was reformed.

What do these hands reaching out suggest about people's initial attitude to the revolution?

A great wind blows the curtain. What was the artist trying to portray by this?

What do you think this man is doing here?

What impression does the painting give about the immediate reaction to the revolution?

Why might they be throwing their hats in the air?

Why do you think this man is sitting like this?

⬆ Drawing by Jacques-Louis David (1791) of the members of the Third Estate making the Tennis Court Oath.

Whom might these three figures represent? Why are they hugging like this?

Activity

1 At the end of this section you will be asked to debate about the significance of the revolution. To do this properly you will need notes on the four criteria from page 92. Copy the criteria as titles on to four different cards.

2 In pairs discuss the questions surrounding picture B. Then you should be able to make some notes on the card about the **immediate impacts** of the revolution. Refer to specific elements of the picture and use the story on pages 92–93 to explain your suggestions.

3 Picture B was made by one of the members of the National Assembly. Can we believe what it is telling us about this event?

What were the effects of the French Revolution?

On the last page you probably made the inference that most people initially thought the revolution was significant. The next six pages visit three periods between 1789 and 1799 to see the effects of the revolution. This will enable us to see if this immediate impact was justified.

When we look at significance we need to consider for *whom* it was significant. We will look at four main groups and their situation before the revolution.

The poor
Had very little money, paid heavy taxes and had no rights under Louis.

Bourgeoisie (middle class)
Had money but were heavily taxed and had no rights under Louis, whom they did not like.

Nobility
Most had lots of money and land, escaped taxes and had rights under Louis and liked him.

The Church
Had lots of money and land, escaped taxes and had rights under Louis.

July 1789–March 1792

A

The August Decrees, 1789

After the events of July, the National Assembly released the following laws:

- tithes (taxes paid to the Church) were abolished
- no positions in government could be sold for money
- all financial and tax privileges were abolished
- all citizens were to be taxed equally
- all citizens were eligible for positions of government.

B

Declaration of the Rights of Man, August 1789

After the August Decrees, the National Assembly also published its principles. The main points were:

- all men are born free and equal in their rights
- power rests with the people
- freedom of worship
- freedom of speech
- freedom to own property.

C

Relief of the poor

The 2 million people who lived in extreme poverty had previously been helped by the Church. But after its land had been sold, the Church could no longer afford this. The Assembly decided it would not take on this role as it also had too little money. Additionally, strikes and **collective bargaining** were made illegal which meant it was impossible to fight for better pay or rights.

D Free trade

The members of the Assembly believed in a **laissez-faire** economy. They removed price controls on grain and later on other products. This meant more profit could be made on these products but prices rose heavily.

E Justice

The Assembly made the law more humane. Torture was abolished and the death penalty was delivered by a new, quicker method – the guillotine.

Justice was free and equal to all.

G Voting

Voting rights were based on how much tax you paid – the more you paid the more power you had.

- Those who paid the equivalent of three days' labour could only vote for the Electors.
- To be an Elector you had to pay the equivalent of ten days' labour which gave you the power to choose the deputies for the Assembly.
- Only those who paid the equivalent of 54 days' labour could actually be a deputy in the Assembly who had the power to make new laws.

Even so, 61 per cent of men had the right to vote which was a massive increase.

F Nationalisation of Church land

Under Louis, the Church was the largest land owner. After the revolution the Assembly needed money. To raise money they forced the Church to sell its land. Anyone with enough money could buy the land. *Assignats*) were given to those who bought the land.

Activity

1 In pairs read through information A to G, which describe the main changes made by the National Assembly. For each piece of evidence discuss how each of the four main groups on page 94 would have been affected on a scale from a very positive effect to a very negative effect.

2 Now discuss on the whole what the overall impact was for each group taking into account all the evidence you discussed in Activity 1. For example, if one group experienced some positive and some negative effects, you will need to make a judgement about whether it was overall more positive or negative.

3 Copy the graph on the right and plot your judgements for each of the four groups for the period **July 1789–March 1792**.

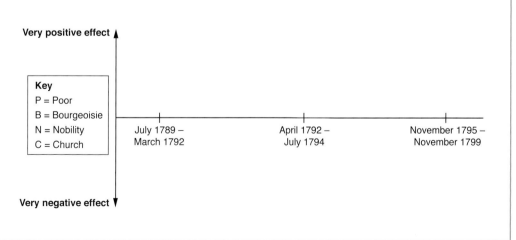

Key
P = Poor
B = Bourgeoisie
N = Nobility
C = Church

Now we will continue the story of the revolution by looking at two further periods: April 1792–July 1794 and November 1795–November 1799.

April 1792–July 1794

The rise of the Commune

In Paris, the urban poor (the **sans-culottes**) had played a pivotal part in leading the revolution, in particular by Storming the Bastille (see page 107). However, they did not receive any benefits from it. They still paid large amounts of tax but had very little political say. As a result they became increasingly **radical** in their ideas and formed political clubs. Forming into a loose group known as the Commune they began calling for a change and in particular, a **Republic**.

In 1789 no one had called for the end of the monarchy but as the years progressed, this changed. Louis was never happy with his role as a **constitutional monarch** but the government remained supportive of him, even when he attempted to flee France and had to be dragged back to Paris in 1791. Everything changed in 1792, however, when the Austrians declared war against the French. Louis stubbornly refused to help with plans to defend Paris and on 10 August the *sans-culottes* had had enough, storming the Tuilleries Palace and arresting Louis.

Fearful for their lives, the supporters of the constitutional monarchy (including many of the nobility) went into hiding. In the new elections in September for the Convention (the new name for the government) **royalists** abstained from voting and all males over 21 were given the vote. The Commune had taken power. In December, at the trial of Louis, they voted to execute him.

> **Think**
>
> Louis' execution was the turning point for how many people perceived the revolution, especially in Britain. Why was this such an important moment in history?

H

⬆ *Execution of Louis XVI*, a German copperplate engraving, 1793, by Georg Heinrich Sieveking.

The Terror

After the execution of Louis, Maximilien Robespierre became the new leader of the government. Faced with war and a public who were angry for change Robespierre and his colleagues believed that the French Revolution needed to take a new path. He created the Committee of Public Safety, a small body of men which essentially ran France as a **dictatorship**. Their eleven-month rule is known as the Terror.

↑ A portrait of Robespierre, c. 1790 (anonymous).

J

Fixed prices

The **General Maximum** fixed the price of goods, including bread, to stop prices rising to the point where people could not afford food anymore. The peasants in the countryside hated this as the price was fixed below the cost it took to produce food; the *sans-culottes* in the towns liked it as they could afford to buy goods. This created a lot of conflict.

K

Robespierre kills the last executioner, 1793. This satirical cartoon implied that Robespierre had killed everyone in France.

L

Execution of rebels

Robespierre set up a large network of spies. Anyone deemed to be against the revolution was sent to their deaths by a Revolutionary Tribunal. Rebels could be killed by the guillotine within 24 hours, and were allowed no jury and no appeal. During the eleven months of the Terror there were 16,600 official executions, but some historians think the real figure is far higher.

Of these deaths 28 per cent were peasants, 31 per cent were *sans-culottes* and only 8 per cent were nobility. Some bourgeois people profited from the death of these people, taking over their businesses.

M

The Revolutionary War

Although war with the rest of Europe had begun before the Terror, the scale of it increased as countries were horrified by what was happening in France. As a result the Committee of Public Safety introduced **conscription** and diverted resources for the army to continue its fight. This meant more food shortages.

The Vendée

In the Vendée region of western France the peasants could not put up with the low prices any more. Rising with some royalist nobles they formed an army to try to overturn the revolution. However, the Revolutionary Army was far stronger and resoundingly crushed them. Of all the deaths in the Terror, half were from the Vendée region alone. Some historians believe as many as 200,000 people might have been killed or executed there.

Think

Look at the faces of the Vendée rebels in picture N. Can you see why this period is called the Terror?

⬆ *La déroute de Cholet* (*The rout at the battle of Cholet*) by Jules Giradet, 1886, shows the rebels trying and failing to escape the Revolutionary Army.

Religion

The *sans-culottes* hated Catholicism as they saw it as a traitor to the revolution as the Catholic Church was so closely associated with the monarchy. As a result the Commune passed laws to de-Christianise France. Churches were closed and crosses destroyed. It is estimated that as many as 20,000 priests were forced to give up their jobs. Robespierre even began his own alternative religion – the '**Cult of the Supreme Being**' – which pleased very few people. On 8 June 1794 he held a festival in the middle of Paris where a man-made 'mountain' was built to celebrate the Supreme Being.

Activity

4 Discuss with a partner what happened during April 1792–July 1794. Which group(s) would have been affected, and would the events have had a positive or negative effect on them?
5 Add the effects for each of the four main groups in **April 1792–July 1794** to your graph.
6 On the next page is what happened in **November 1795–November 1799**. Read this and plot on your graph how each of the groups were affected in this final period.

November 1795–November 1799

By July 1794 Robespierre's enemies had had enough. He was arrested and executed, along with 100 other members of the Commune. A new government began, the Directory, run by the bourgeoisie who had bought land or office in the years 1789–92. They:

- abolished the Revolutionary Tribunal and released many of its prisoners
- re-established freedom of religious worship and ended the Cult of the Supreme Being
- abolished price controls (which meant prices rose steeply); when the *sans-culottes* protested at bread prices they were crushed
- introduced new taxes, in particular on land (this lasted until 1914)
- introduced a new constitution which gave the vote to all males over 21 who paid taxes (although real power still lay with the Electors – who now had to pay tax equivalent to 150 to 200 days' work!)
- crushed royalists who protested for the return of a monarch.

All good stories have a twist at the end (like television soaps) and often end on a cliff hanger. The French Revolution was no different.

During the years 1795 to 1799 the army had become increasingly angry at the Directory which was not funding them sufficiently to win the Revolutionary War (see page 98). In 1799 a general who had won a number of notable battles, Napoleon Bonaparte, took power in a **coup d'etat**, getting rid of the Directory and establishing his own rule.

◀ *General Bonaparte during the coup d'état of 18 Brumaire in Saint-Cloud*, by François Bouchot, 1840.

Look back at picture B on page 93.

Activity

7 In pairs discuss the following question:

   Who were the real winners and losers of the French Revolution?

8 Look back at picture B on page 93. As a class, discuss if you think their reactions were justified. If they had known what was coming would they have looked so happy?

9 You should now have lots of evidence from your discussion and your graph to think about how significant the French Revolution was in the short term. Complete the **short-term effects** card from page 92. Remember to mention the impact on each of the four groups you have been looking at in this chapter, referring to specific evidence.

Think

1 What do you think is going to happen next to France?
2 Use picture P to think about what type of man it shows Napoleon to be.

Should you have a bust of Napoleon in your classroom?

When the author of this section was a child his father bought him a bust of Napoleon, who was one of his heroes. When Mr Kennett became a teacher he wanted to put this in his classroom but his colleagues and friends – who did not admire Napoleon – told him off and said this was wrong!

Now, nearly 200 years after his death, Napoleon is still a very controversial figure. To some he is the saviour of the French Revolution; to others its destroyer. To truly see the permanence of the revolution we need to look at what happened between 1800 and 1815. As we do this you should decide if you think Mr Kennett should have a bust of Napolean in his classroom or not.

As you have just seen there are very different interpretations of Napoleon. The next two pictures reveal the two main interpretations people have. These help to explain why Napoleon remains so controversial.

⬆ The author Mr Kennett with his bust of Napoleon.

⬅ *Napoleon crossing the Alps* by Jacques-Louis David, a French artist, 1801. It was commissioned by the Spanish King as a present for Napoleon. The scene commemorates Napoleon's victory over the area that is now north Italy.

Enquiry Step 1: First evidence – asking questions

1 Why do you think that people have such different reactions to a man who lived over 200 years ago?

2 What questions does it make you want to ask about Napoleon?

↑ *Maniac ravings or Little Boney* [a nickname for Napoleon Bonaparte] *in a strong fit* by James Gillray, 1803. Gillray was a British artist and this caricature was produced a week after the British had gone to war with the French.

Enquiry Step 2: Suggesting an answer

Look carefully at pictures B and C.

1 Write down any adjectives (descriptive words) you might use to describe the way that Napoleon is represented in each of these pictures.

2 Why do you think these two artists portrayed Napoleon so differently? What is the purpose of each of these images? Can we believe the message of either of them?

3 Write down your initial thoughts in answer to the enquiry question:

Should you have a bust of Napoleon in your classroom?

Hero or villain?

As pictures B and C (pages 100–101) show, Napoleon is either seen as a saviour of the revolution (the hero) or the destroyer of the revolution (the villain), which is why he has remained so controversial. Your challenge now is to work out which of these interpretations is more accurate.

D

Napoleon created a new nobility to help keep people loyal to him. Between 1808 and 1814, 3,500 new titles were given, including new dukes and barons. These people received large estates of land.

E

The **direct tax** system was reformed and controlled centrally which allowed for successful collection.

G

The ordinary people were very repressed. There was a large police force who spied on them and in 1810 a new law meant that you could be put in prison without trial.

F

In 1800 the Bank of France was created. It established a new stable currency, the franc.

H

Censorship increased greatly. In 1809 censors were appointed to each newspaper and in 1810 the number of printing presses was reduced by half.

I

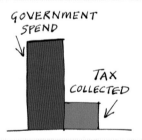

GOVERNMENT SPEND

TAX COLLECTED

There was still a large gap between the amount the government spent and the amount of taxes it collected.

J

Napoleon was made Emperor in 1804. He had complete control in peace and war. In all matters his decision was final.

K

New **indirect taxes** were introduced which hurt the poorest, including a tax on salt, something the revolutionaries had fought hard against in 1789. Revenue from these taxes increased 400 per cent between 1806 and 1812.

L

Napoleon acted like a king. He was crowned by the Pope in 1804 and the French decided to give him hereditary power meaning that when he died his son would be the next ruler.

M

Napoleon created the Grande Armée. This was a modern army with good leadership and tactics.

N

The 1804 *Code Napoléon* reorganised the law, bringing all the different laws into one system, making it a lot more effective. However, it also re-established slavery.

O

New secondary schools were set up (lycéés). These were very good but were only for the sons of soldiers or government officials.

P

Universal suffrage was established in France. But the election process was very complicated meaning power was restricted to a select few.

Q

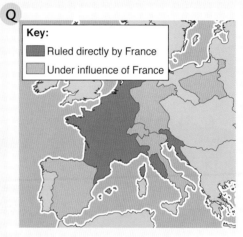

Key:
- Ruled directly by France
- Under influence of France

In 1812 the French Empire stretched over most of Europe.

Enquiry Step 3: Developing your answer

Read evidence D–Q and copy the table below.

1 Working with a partner or in a small group categorise the evidence into the following categories: Politics, Economy, Society or Warfare. Write the letters of the evidence into the first column (P, E, S or W).

2 For each category (Politics, Economy, Society and Warfare) re-read the evidence. Decide if overall it shows Napoleon to be a hero or a villain. Write your judgement into the second column.

	Evidence of Napoleon's impact (add the letters of the relevant pieces of evidence below)	Was Napoleon a hero or villain in this aspect? Explain your opinion below
Politics		
Economy		
Society		
Warfare		

How did things change after 1812?

If this story had ended in 1812 we might have quite a different picture of Napoleon. He had conquered most of Europe (see map Q on page 103) and the French economy was booming. However, by 1815 things had changed quite a lot.

Read the facts on pages 104–105 to see if they change your opinion of Napoleon, before reaching a final conclusion about whether or not the author Mr Kennett should have a bust of Napoleon in his classroom.

1812

Napoleon, greedy with power, decided to invade Russia. However, the French were not prepared for the winter or the fierce Russians. Although they reached Moscow, the Grande Armée was reduced from 400,000 to 40,000 from death or illness.

⬆ Napoleon's army was devastated by the Russian winter.

October 1813

The Coalition (Russia, Prussia, Austria, Britain, Spain and Sweden) teamed up to beat Napoleon and had a series of successes, notably at the Battle of Leipzig, the largest battle in history at this time.

⬆ Russians, Prussians and Austrians meet after the first decisive defeat of Napoleon.

April 1814

Napoleon was surrounded. Admitting defeat, he was exiled to the tiny island of Elba, off the coast of Italy.

February 1815

Napoleon escaped and went back to France! Surrounded by crowds shouting 'Vive L'Empereur!' he triumphantly returned to Paris.

⬆ Napoleon's troops were overjoyed by his return.

15 June 1815

With the Coalition in modern-day Belgium, Napoleon took a 200,000 strong Grande Armée and secretly crossed the border to face them for one last time.

16 June 1815

Initial battles against the British (Quatre Bras) and the Prussians (Ligny) were French successes. The British managed to retreat to the village of Waterloo. The Prussians regrouped and planned what to do next.

⬆ By the evening of the 16th, Napoleon took advantage.

18 June 1815

The British led by the Duke of Wellington awaited the French at Waterloo for the battle to end all battles. Rain overnight had left the field muddy. As a result Napoleon held off the fighting until midday. All afternoon the British held the ridge using clever infantry and cavalry manoeuvres. When hope was fading in early evening the Prussians led by Blücher arrived and together the British and Prussians beat Napoleon. Twenty-eight years of war were over.

⬆ Napoleon was defeated at Waterloo.

July 1815 onwards

Napoleon gave in for the final time. He was exiled to St Helena, an island in the south Atlantic, where he died in 1821. In France, Louis XVIII was restored to the throne.

Enquiry Step 4: Concluding your enquiry

1 By now you should have a really good idea about whether Napoleon was a hero or a villain. Working on your own, write a response about whether you think Mr Kennett should or should not display the bust of Napoleon in his classroom. Explain your opinion.

2 Napoleon's reign really shows the significance of the French Revolution in the medium term as he is a product of the revolution. Were there any positive impacts from Napoleon's rule or was he all maniac, like the Gillray cartoon on page 101 shows? Write down your thoughts about this on the **medium-term effects** card.

Was the French Revolution significant in the long term?

We started off this section by saying that one measure of the significance of the French Revolution is how long its effects lasted. To judge this we are going to take a sneaky peak ahead to the rest of the nineteenth century and beyond, both in France and elsewhere.

> France is still a republic, something we are very proud of!

2015 – a distant relation

In France

The years 1815 to 1870 were a period of rapid change in France. A Frenchman who lived through these years could tell us what happened. His story will show us if the effects of the revolution were permanent.

> Monarchy has been restored! Louis XVI's brother, also called Louis, is going to be our new king – Louis XVIII. He will rule as a constitutional monarch.

> In 1848 France had yet again another revolution, where the **Orleans monarchy** was got rid of and replaced by the Second Republic. However, this only managed to last three years before Louis Napoleon (Bonaparte's nephew) established himself as Napoleon III in 1851.

1815   1830   1851   1870

> Another year, another revolution! The old **Bourbon monarchy** has been overthrown and replaced with the **Orleans monarchy**. Another constitutional monarch.

> People were angry that France was losing wars throughout Europe and rose up again in 1870 against Napoleon III. The Third Republic was set up in 1870 without a monarchy. We all hope it will last. Vive la France!

Think

Does this story show that the French Revolution set France on a path towards a permanent republic, or was it just a random chaotic series of events that led to this?

Additionally the revolution left its mark on France and Europe in other ways too …

All of Europe drives on the right – this was forced upon countries by Napoleon.

The metric system of litres, kilometres and kilograms – this was created to give consistency to the French Empire. It is now used throughout the world.

Bastille Day – every 14 July the French celebrate the Storming of the Bastille with a national holiday and fireworks.

The baguette – this was a Napoleonic invention to make it easy for troops to carry bread in their bags.

Elsewhere

It was not just in France that the French Revolution had an impact. Below are three characters who will tell you about its impact further afield.

The revolution inspired people like me to fight for liberty and equality throughout Europe. Those of us at Peterloo (see page 42) fighting for the vote were directly inspired by the French. This movement for the extension of the franchise led to the mass democracy of your present day.

The Revolutionary Wars with France brought a new form of modern warfare to Europe. British generals like me learned a lot during these wars and developed techniques and technology we could use to dominate the world!

The French Revolution and Napoleon showed what it meant to be a modern-day nation state. This made others think about nationalism and led people like the members of Young Ireland (see page 70) to fight for their nation.

Activity

1 What does the story on page 106 show about how permanent the effects of the revolution were in nineteenth-century France? Was there a revolutionary legacy?
2 Does the content of page 107 show the French Revolution was of greater or lesser significance in France or outside of France? Explain your answer.
3 This chapter should have given you a really good idea about how permanent the effects of the revolution were. Add your overall judgement to the **long-term effects** card.

Pulling it all together: How significant was the French Revolution?

So far in this section we have looked at what happened in France and elsewhere as a result of the French Revolution. You will agree that it is a topsy-turvy history and that it is difficult to reach a clear conclusion about its significance. Historians still cannot agree about its significance today.

How has opinion changed about the French Revolution?

The Marxist interpretation (Georges Lefebvre)

Historians of the early twentieth century (such as the French historian Lefebvre) saw the revolution as the key moment of modern history – a moment of social revolution when the people overthrew the old nobility, and when the bourgeoisie took control and began to turn France into a capitalist society.

The revisionist interpretation (Alfred Cobban)

In the 1960s historians began to question the Marxist view of the revolution. Alfred Cobban (a British historian) argued that feudal society had disappeared long before 1789, and that the revolution actually did little to change the everyday lives of the people.

Instead, Cobban portrayed the revolution as a political revolution, in which the old inefficient monarchy was replaced by the more modern Napoleonic state.

The post-revisionist interpretation (Simon Schama)

In the late 1980s, the 200th anniversary of the revolution resulted in lots of new books being written.

One of the most successful was Simon Schama's *Citizens*. He denied that there was any 'grand historical design' behind the events of the revolution, and instead presented it as a chaotic series of reactions to events, a jumble of distinct, local revolutions, which lost its way and descended into violence.

Schama (a British historian) is part of a British tradition of interpretation of the French Revolution, which sees the revolution at best as an irrelevance and at worst as a disaster.

> **Think**
>
> Which of these three interpretations might be summed up with each of the following phrases:
> 1 social change
> 2 political change
> 3 negative change?

Activity

1 In a small group decide which interpretation on page 108 you agree with most. Share this with your class and as a whole class agree which interpretation makes most sense.

2 E.H. Carr, a very famous historian, said that to understand an interpretation we must understand the context in which it is written. Below are some facts about the context of the three interpretations on the left. In pairs match two facts with each interpretation. To find the correct answers go to page i.

A
This historian was writing just after the Russian Revolution when communism and **Marxism** were still popular.

B
This historian was writing at the time of the bicentenary of the French Revolution.

C
This historian was writing during the Cold War. Academics turned away from Marxism as it was associated with the Soviets whom the West was 'fighting'.

D
This historian came from a wealthy background. He was interested in economics and politics.

E
This historian was writing at a time when there was negative feeling in Britain towards the European Union and the French.

F
This historian came from a poor background and as a result was interested in the history of class struggle.

3 Go back to your small group. Discuss whether this new knowledge about these interpretations changes your opinion about which interpretation you most agree with.

4 Now you are going to take your own part in this debate and produce a piece of extended writing to show your own opinion on:

How significant was the French Revolution?

▌ Start by writing a paragraph about the importance of the impact of the French Revolution at the time, using the ideas you have gathered on your **immediate impact** card.

▌ Then write a paragraph about what was changed by 1799, using the ideas you have gathered on your **short-term effects** card, remembering to mention how each of the four groups were affected differently.

▌ Next, write a paragraph about the **medium-term effects** of the revolution, considering if Napoleon had a positive or negative impact on France.

▌ Your next paragraph will be a discussion of how permanent the effects of the revolution were and if they still affect us today. Use the ideas you have gathered on your **long-term effects** card.

▌ Finally, write a conclusion. What do you ultimately think about the significance of the French Revolution? Explain your decision, taking into account the interpretations of different historians, and evaluating which interpretations you think are accurate and which you think are not.

Slums, smog and sewers? What was the big story of change, 1745–1901?

Throughout this series of books so far you have examined how big historical events impacted upon and changed the lives of ordinary people. In this section you will investigate one of the biggest changes in British history, the **Industrial Revolution**. In doing so you will consider whether this story was simply one of slums, smog and sewers or if there was a little more to it.

Think

Manchester in 1844 was known as 'Cottonopolis' due to its position as the main textile producing centre in the world. This painting is called *Manchester from Kersal Moor* by William Wylde (1857). What do you think the artist was trying to say about the city?

In 1844 the German philosopher Friedrich Engels went to live in the northern English city of Manchester. Engels would go on to work with another philosopher, Karl Marx, to develop the political theory known as Marxism. This theory argues that eventually ordinary working people will grow tired of living in poverty and rise up in a violent revolution that will change the world. Some of these ideas developed when Engels was living in Manchester. This is how he described what he saw there:

350,000 working people of Manchester and its environs live, almost all of them, in wretched, damp, filthy cottages. The streets around them are usually in the most miserable and filthy condition.

Was Engels right?

It would be easy for us to simply accept Engels' view of life in industrial Manchester as being representative of the entire period of 1745–1901, the period in which Britain went through the huge changes of the Industrial Revolution.

But was he correct? Historians have been debating the impact of the Industrial Revolution almost since it began. Historians at the start of the twentieth century always saw the story of the changes in the lives of ordinary people as simply one of misery.

Later, in the 1960s and 1970s, the debate was split between 'optimists' who saw improvements in among the changes and 'pessimists' who clung to the idea that life remained a grind for ordinary people. Eventually, historians began to realise that ordinary life clearly had improved and so this debate became one of 'when' did these improvements begin.

In this section you will enter into the debate and overview the changes to the lives of ordinary people across the period 1745–1901. You will examine life in rural Britain and then contrast it with life in the cities. Finally you will focus upon some specific case studies. By the end you will have a clear view of what changed, how and why it changed, and will be able to make some decisions about how you would describe these changes.

Activity

1 Make a copy of the table below. Read pages 112–13 about life for ordinary people in 1745. Record details onto the first column of your table.

Aspects of life	1745	1850	1901
Housing			
Work			
Education			
Leisure and travel			
Health			

2 As you read pages 114–17 on life for ordinary people in 1850 and 1901 note down any improvements in one colour, what got worse in another colour and any examples of no change in a third colour.

3 Once your table is completed you will be able to answer the following questions.
   a) Was there any truth to the types of living conditions Engels described?
   b) Was Engel's viewpoint representative of the entire period from 1745 to 1901?
   c) What do you think the most important changes were during this period? Compare your list with that of your partner. (Don't forget to explain your choices.)
   d) Were there any features of life in this period that you feel did not change? Give examples.

Britain 1745

Housing

As most people lived in the countryside, housing for ordinary people was mainly farming cottages. These would be of brick and wood construction, often with thatched roofs. Cottages would often have their own small plot of land for the growing of vegetables and keeping of poultry. Clothing would be almost entirely home spun, from locally produced flax or wool.

Health

With medical knowledge only at a very basic level, Britain in 1745 had a high **infant mortality rate**. Many children did not survive their first year. The annual death rate was 28 per 1,000 people with most ordinary people having a life expectancy of around 40 years. This high death rate was in part due to a lack of medical knowledge. People in 1745 had no idea that germs were a major cause of illness and there were no antibiotics or anaesthetics. Surgery was a very risky business with many people dying of shock, blood loss or infection. Food was home grown, with most farming families living on bread, butter, tea and potatoes. Many people lived with the threat of hunger and starvation if harvests were poor. In 1740–41 there had been famine in Ireland caused by the failure of the harvest.

⬆ *Haymaking in rural Hampshire Meadows*, James Edwin.

Work

With 80 per cent of the population (about 11 million people) living in the countryside the main occupation was farming – the growing of food and the rearing of livestock for meat, milk, wool and leather. The manufacture of clothing was done using the **domestic system**. This meant that the majority of textile manufacture was done at home with various members of the family taking part in the spinning and weaving process. As well as farming and textile work there was also small-scale manufacturing in workshops, making items such as barrels, bridles, nails and cutlery, as well as some mining and metal work.

Leisure and travel
Ordinary working people in 1745 enjoyed fewer holidays than workers in the Middle Ages. This was due to the Protestant Church banning the old Saints Day holidays of the Catholic Church. Most people would work a six-day week, with only Sunday as a day of rest and church attendance. Travel was mainly on foot or by horse. As a result of this, and the state of many of the roads, journey times were long. Even with the improvements made by turnpike roads (where people would buy up sections of road, improve them and then charge people to use them), journey times were lengthy. A journey from London to Edinburgh in 1745 could take twelve days.

Education
In 1745 education was mainly reserved for the children of the rich. Very few ordinary people could read or write, with any school attendance being for only one or two years. Dame Schools existed for ordinary people. These were usually held in the home of the teacher and provided boys and girls with an education of variable quality ranging from a glorified baby-sitting service to schools that provided the basics of reading and writing. By the late 1750s there was a Sunday school movement, aimed at providing basic education and Christian values to boys in slum areas of the cities. There were a total of seven universities in Britain. All students at these universities were male.

The Big Picture

9 Slums, smog and sewers? What was the big story of change, 1745–1901?

Britain 1850

Housing
In rural parts of Britain housing had not really changed in the years since 1745. However, due to the growth in industry offering jobs in factories, mills and mines, more of the population (about 50 per cent) were now living in towns and cities. Housing in towns and cities such as Leeds, Newcastle, Glasgow and Manchester was often of poor quality. It was overcrowded, tightly packed, badly constructed and with no running water, drains or toilets. Many families lived in single room flats with only very basic furniture. Even beds were often shared, with different members of the family sleeping at different times according to their shifts at the factory, mill or mine.

Education
A decent education was mostly the privilege of the wealthy upper and middle classes. Ordinary, working-class people were often reluctant to spend their hard-earned wages on educating their children. There was no compulsory, free education for children. Some Dame Schools continued to function although a report in 1838 suggested that the quality of education remained variable. For the wealthy, there were several universities but these were off-limits to the ordinary members of the public.

⬆ Wentworth Works, a file and steel manufacturers and exporter of iron, in Sheffield, c.1860.

Health

Knowledge of germs and medical theory in general remained unchanged since 1745. There were still no antibiotics and no anaesthetics, meaning surgery was still a risky venture. Although a vaccination against smallpox had been developed, saving many lives, there were still many killer diseases. In the overcrowded slums typhoid, tuberculosis and **cholera** were major killers. A cholera epidemic in 1848–49 killed around 50,000 people. As a water-borne disease cholera travelled quickly in Britain's overcrowded cities. Infant mortality remained high, and while the overall death rate had fallen to 22 per 1,000 people, life expectancy in the towns and cities was down to 35 years. Thanks to better farming and improved transport links cheaper food began to become more readily available to ordinary people.

Work

By 1851, the total population stood at 27.5 million. While half of the working population continued to be employed in the countryside doing farming related jobs, half were also working in towns and cities. Britain in this period saw a huge growth in jobs in factories (for example, the mills of Lancashire and Yorkshire), mining (such as in the north-east of England) and on the railways. Working hours were typically long – sometimes up to twelve hours per day – but wages were often better than could be earned in farming jobs. However, the Factory Acts of 1833 and 1844 (see page 125) had begun to reduce the hours that children were allowed to work. Thanks to machinery there was less demand for skilled workers and this did lead to unemployment in some areas. There was no safety net for those who became unemployed – no pensions, no unemployment benefits and no sick pay.

Leisure and travel

With the majority of ordinary city workers tied to the hours and shifts of the mines and factories, holidays were a rarity. People generally continued to work six-day weeks with Sundays off. The expansion of the railways was well under way by 1850 and this was cutting journey times around the country. The journey from London to Edinburgh in 1850 would take twelve and a half hours. These improvements in rail transport not only benefited industry but also allowed a reliable postal service to be developed.

Britain 1901

Health

By 1901 the annual death rate had fallen to eighteen deaths per 1,000 people. This improvement was also matched by a fall in the rate of infant mortality. Thanks to the work of Louis Pasteur, doctors now knew that germs were a cause of illness and vaccinations against many previously deadly diseases had been developed. Similarly, the development of anaesthetics and increased awareness of the need for hygiene had greatly increased the chances of surviving an operation.

Improvements in refrigeration had made the transport of food more efficient. However, the poor health of recruits for the Boer Wars in 1899 and 1900 suggest that the diet of ordinary people remained limited.

Education

The overall level of education for ordinary British people had improved by 1901. Following Education Acts in 1870 every child had to attend elementary school between the ages of five and ten. This meant that many more people were able to read and write. For those who could afford it, there were a total of seventeen universities in Britain. These were now open to women at an undergraduate level. This means women could study for the most basic level of university degree.

⬆ Featherstone Main Pit, West Yorkshire, early 1900s.

Leisure and travel

People continued to work long hours but it was becoming more common to have Saturday afternoon off work. This allowed people to enjoy sporting activities and to watch cricket and football matches. The first official football club was Sheffield Wednesday, set up in 1857. Since 1871, the Bank Holiday Act had protected workers' holidays, allowing people to have holidays on Boxing Day, Easter Monday, Whit Monday and the first Monday in August. By 1900 Britain boasted over 18,000 miles of railway lines which allowed people to take breaks to beach resorts such as Brighton, Southend and Blackpool. Travel times continued to fall, with more people owning cars and with faster trains. By 1900 the journey from London to Edinburgh took nine hours.

Housing

By 1901 a massive 75 per cent of the population lived in towns and cities. The quality of new housing in Britain had generally improved. Builders of new houses had to follow government and local council regulations in order to improve drainage and ventilation. At the same time, following the great cholera outbreaks there had been efforts made by local councils to improve sewer systems and public water supplies. However, old housing problems remained with slum areas persisting in many big cities. Studies by social reformers such as Rowntree and Booth in the 1890s revealed that millions of British people still lived in squalid, overcrowded housing. This situation would only begin to be addressed after the general election of 1906 when the newly elected Liberals undertook to bring in laws to help the poor.

Work

Only 25 per cent of the working population, which numbered around 40 million by 1901, still worked in the countryside. While animal power was still used on farms there were also machines to make farmers' working lives a little easier. Factories and mines now regularly used steam power, with Britain still leading the world in heavy industry such as textiles, mining and shipbuilding. For people in need there was still no unemployment benefit, nor could people claim sick pay or receive pensions.

9

Slums, smog and sewers? What was the big story of change, 1745–1901?

Change in the countryside – how would we best describe changes in the village of Ashill?

When we think of historical change it is sometimes tempting to think that it happened like a person flicking a light switch on. One moment the room was dark, the next it was illuminated. In this chapter you will examine the nature of change in one small rural village. You will look at the factors leading to change and we will try to expand the vocabulary we use when describing historical change.

Between 1745 and 1825 some huge changes occurred. The number of people living in Britain during this period almost doubled, and as you have seen, the growth of new industries began to change how and where people worked. With a rising population and new industrial cities to feed, Britain needed to produce a lot more food. This need for more food led to changes, not only in farming techniques, but also in the lives of the people who lived and worked in the countryside, such as those who lived in the village of Ashill.

A

The strip system of farming has to go. You villagers divide all of your fields into strips and farm them how you wish. This is an incredibly wasteful system. Crops are being grown on different strips, and between each strip is a pathway, meaning less land is cultivated.

The idea of common land is very wasteful. Having a huge area of the village left uncultivated just so villagers can graze a few cattle is a ridiculous waste of land. I want the land enclosed. I will apply to Parliament for the right to take over the common land and put it to better use, growing food for Britain.

I've been thinking a lot about our lack of machinery. There are some wonderful innovations being made in farming technology. We need to start using these on our land here. From seed drills to new ploughs, we have lots of new machines that could be used in Ashill to help us produce more food.

This 'three field rotation system' worries me. **Fallow fields** are terribly wasteful. If one field in every three is left empty then a third of our growing potential is gone every year. Gone! Viscount Townsend has been doing wonderful things: planting turnips and using a clay called marl as a fertiliser to enrich his soil and cultivate more land. This is what Ashill needs – innovation!

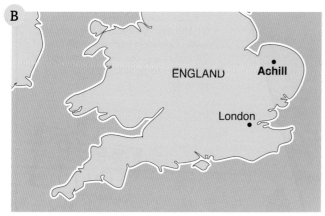

↑ A map showing the location of the village of Ashill. Between 1785 and 1870, Ashill, like many villages in Britain, went through a considerable period of change, in what some historians have called an Agricultural Revolution.

Activity

Study picture A below. It is an artist's impression of the big landowner in Ashill explaining to one of his tenants in 1780 why things needed to change. As you read the conversation make a list of all of the arguments being put forward about why things in Ashill needed to change.

The strip system allows every villager to work to the best of their ability. But I agree it is difficult to grow a lot of food. Also, as the strips are regularly swapped it stops people from wanting to improve the quality of their strip. Why work hard to improve land that you can't guarantee will be yours next year?

But villagers have a right to use the common land. We don't just graze a few cows; we use the commons for **gleaning**. If we lose it you will be depriving people of a way to supplement their income and help their families.

Machines all sound very nice sir, but won't that mean lots of the villagers will lose out on work? A lot of our autumn work comes from jobs we do once the farming year is over – **threshing corn**, for example, and getting it ready for the flour mills. If we introduce machines, what will people do instead?

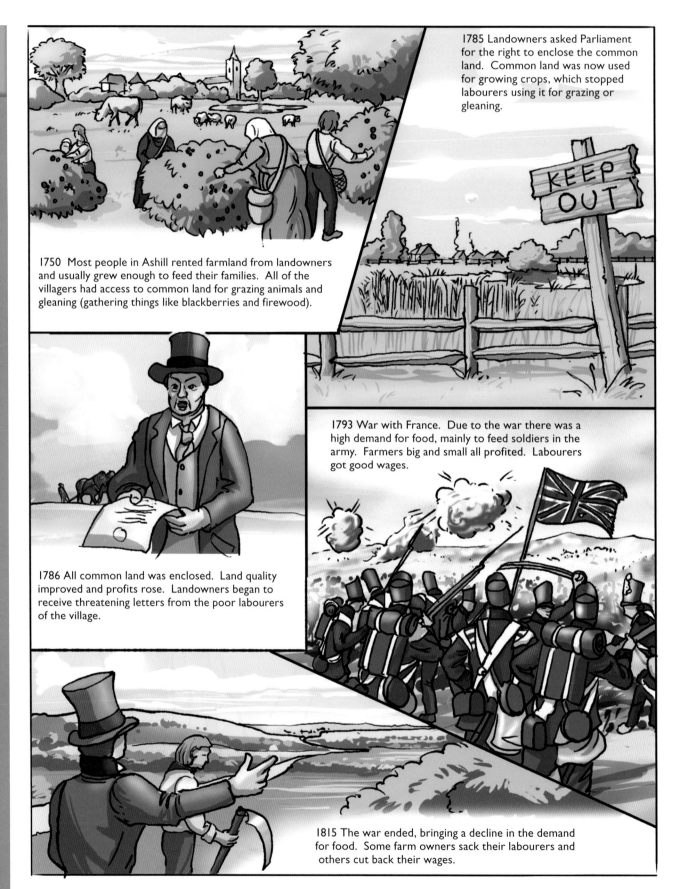

9

Slums, smog and sewers? What was the big story of change, 1745–1901?

1785 Landowners asked Parliament for the right to enclose the common land. Common land was now used for growing crops, which stopped labourers using it for grazing or gleaning.

KEEP OUT

1750 Most people in Ashill rented farmland from landowners and usually grew enough to feed their families. All of the villagers had access to common land for grazing animals and gleaning (gathering things like blackberries and firewood).

1786 All common land was enclosed. Land quality improved and profits rose. Landowners began to receive threatening letters from the poor labourers of the village.

1793 War with France. Due to the war there was a high demand for food, mainly to feed soldiers in the army. Farmers big and small all profited. Labourers got good wages.

1815 The war ended, bringing a decline in the demand for food. Some farm owners sack their labourers and others cut back their wages.

1830 Landowners introduced threshing machines, speeding up food production, meaning bigger profits. Machines also took away the main winter work for many farm labourers.

1831 The Swing Riots. Farm labourers attacked landowners' farms and destroyed threshing machines. Many farms were firebombed. Eventually the authorities cracked down on the rioters and many ringleaders were transported to Australia or hanged.

1834 The Poor Law was changed. Instead of unemployed farm labourers being given bread and money they were sent to live in a poor house. Families were split up.

1850 Rising population caused a big demand for food. Farm owners and labourers made good money.

Town 15miles

1870 British farmers suffered from competition from farmers in America and Australia. Prices fell and many people left Ashill in search of factory work in the towns.

Activity

From 1795–1870 things in Ashill did begin to change. Draw a graph. On the x axis put the dates 1750, 1800, 1850, 1870; on the y axis put 'life is a struggle' at the bottom. 'Life is okay' in the middle and 'Life is good' at the top. As you read the cartoon strip detailing the changes in the village plot your graph.

1 What were the main changes in this period?
2 Did ordinary people's lives get better, worse or was it a mix of the two?
3 How would you describe the changes that took place in Ashill? Read the advice box below to help you with this task.

Advice

Improving your writing about change and continuity!

Try to avoid simply describing the changes you have seen as 'quick' or 'slow'. You have an opportunity here to improve your historical vocabulary and to think very carefully about the nature of historical change. Below are listed some words that you can use to describe the changes you graphed.

▮ Rapid: Change happened at a very fast pace.
▮ Gradual: Change was at a slow pace, perhaps even glacial, if the change was very slow, like the creeping movement of a glacier.

▮ Non-existent: Change did not happen at all.
▮ Progress: Things generally got better for ordinary people.
▮ Regress: Things generally got worse for ordinary people.
▮ Uneven: There was a mixture of progress and regress.
▮ Oscillating: Change went quickly back and forward between progress and regress.
▮ Partial: Changes did not affect everyone.

9

Slums, smog and sewers? What was the big story of change, 1745–1901?

Urbanisation – would moving to Manchester in 1850 have been a change for the better?

One of the things that went hand in hand with Britain becoming a more industrial nation was that lots of people made the decision to move from rural, farming communities such as Ashill to the fast growing industrial towns and cities.

Do you think that this would have been an easy decision for people to make? What would you have done? If 'slums, smog and sewers' is an accurate description for this period then moving from countryside to city would seem a foolish idea. In this chapter you will examine the pros and cons of life in the industrial cities. At the end, on page 125, you will have acquired the knowledge to answer an important historical question: is change always for the better?

On the surface, the question of moving from a quiet country village to the hustle and stink of a big city like Manchester could appear to be an easy decision to make. Compare pictures A and B below. On the left is an artist's impression of a farm worker's cottage, on the right an artist's impression of a cellar dwelling occupied by textile workers in Manchester.

A

B

Think

What words would you use to describe these two paintings?

Which one seems the most pleasant looking?

Where would you prefer to live?

As historians we know that it is unwise to make decisions based upon only a few pieces of evidence; we need the full story. Before we examine the pros and cons of life in industrial Manchester, we will start by examining what might have prompted someone to leave the countryside. These reasons are often called push factors by historians and geographers.

A short summary of rural life

Workers in the countryside often faced a hard life with low wages. Farm workers in Dorset, for example, in 1846 rarely earned more than seven shillings (35 pence) per week. Shepherds lived lives of virtual isolation for long periods of time and might have to spend up to a week travelling and sleeping outside just to get their sheep to market. Job security for farm labourers was almost unknown as they could be sacked at a moment's notice and those who did find themselves unemployed would be forced to stand in line at the nearest hiring fair in the hope of getting a new job.

In contrast to the cosy farm cottage you saw in pictures A and B, have a look at extract C, a description of a village in 1846.

C

> A stream composed of the matter which constantly escapes from pigsties and other receptacles of filth, meanders down each street, being here and there collected into standing pools, which lie festering and rotting in the sun.
>
> *The Illustrated London News in 1846.*

The same newspaper mentions that most labourers and their families lived mostly on bread and describes their cottages as hovels. It concludes that:

> *… want, famine and misery are the features of the village.*

These living and working conditions were not helped by wider changes and events affecting the countryside. For example, the introduction of threshing machines (see page 119) had taken away winter employment from many farm labourers, leading to seasonal unemployment. Moreover, the 1840s were a particularly bad decade for the farmers of Britain and Ireland.

Activity

1 Summarise the problems facing farm labourers.
2 Which problem do you think would provide the biggest 'push' to encourage someone to move to the cities? Explain your reasoning.
3 We now need to examine the alternative to farm life that a move to a city like Manchester would entail. Would moving to Manchester in 1850 really have been a change for the better for rural workers?
   Make a copy of the table below. As you read through pages 124–125 record evidence of the pros and cons of living and working in Manchester.

Positive aspects of living in Manchester	Negative aspects of living in Manchester

9

Slums, smog and sewers? What was the big story of change, 1745–1901?

Manchester 1850

The city of Manchester grew rapidly during the period 1745–1850. From a population of 18,000 in 1750 Manchester boasted 303,000 people by 1851. This growth was largely thanks to the cotton industry. Ideally placed geographically, the city had just the right climate for cotton mills. The damp air of north-west England ensured that cotton did not dry out and snap while it was worked. Rail and canal links to Liverpool meant goods could be quickly imported and exported via the ports and the area was close to the coal fields of Lancashire to provide power for mills and factories.

In this industrial powerhouse, jobs could be plentiful and varied. Pictures D, E and F below show workers employed around Manchester; note the variety of jobs available and the fact that these workers were male and female, young and old.

⬇ Workers in Manchester: (top) outside a cotton mill; (bottom left) household staff; (bottom right) at the gasworks.

D

E

F

124

The job opportunities offered in Manchester were not just limited to the cotton mills, although these were a major employer. Manchester offered work in factories, warehouses, chemical plants as well as on the canals and railways along with jobs as diverse as chimney sweeps, office work and domestic service. Thanks to the rapid expansion of machinery, factory work was often low skilled – ideal for people who had migrated to Manchester from farming jobs. Mill and factory work typically earned a worker twelve shillings (60 pence) per week, for twelve-hour day shifts.

For those who found themselves working in the factories and cotton mills, long twelve-hour days were the norm and factory discipline was strict. As cotton mills often employed children there was a desire to make them conform to the requirements of the job by imposing upon them a set of rules and fines.

Offence	Fines
Any spinner found with his window open	1 shilling
Any spinner found dirty at his work	1 shilling
Any spinner found washing himself	1 shilling
Any spinner heard whistling	1 shilling
Any spinner being 5 minutes late	1 shilling
Any spinner having a little waste on his spindles	1 shilling
Any spinner being sick and cannot find another spinner (to replace him)	6 shillings

As well as the fines imposed on workers, there was also the ever-present threat of beatings and injuries. In 1831, Elizabeth Bentley, a 23-year-old cotton mill worker, gave evidence to a Parliamentary enquiry. Her testimony described her constantly being on her feet, carrying heavy loads, breathing in cotton dust which damaged her lungs and being beaten if she did not work fast enough. Possibly the worst thing the owners could do to a worker was to sack them. With no unemployment benefit, being jobless presented a real danger.

For Manchester's children one change for the better had appeared in 1844 with the passing of the Factory Act. This Act of Parliament had limited the working hours of children aged 8–13 to a total of six and a half per day.

With a rising population, Manchester needed houses for its workers. The quality of this housing was often poor. The communist writer Friedrich Engels (see page 39), who lived in Manchester, described typical workers' houses in the following terms:

> *Heaps of refuse, offal and sickening filth are everywhere … A horde of ragged women and children swarm about the streets and they are just as filthy as the pigs which wallow happily on the heaps of garbage … On average 20 people lived in each of these little houses … One privy [toilet] is shared by about 120 people.*

The inhabitants of these houses lived mainly on a diet of bread, porridge, tea, potatoes and sometimes bacon. Thanks to the building of the Liverpool–Manchester railway, coal for heating houses became cheaper and more readily available. However, the burning of coal, along with the smoke from factories, combined to make Manchester a heavily polluted city.

Like other developing industrial cities in 1850, Manchester also had a growing middle class. These were the owners of the city's businesses. Their houses, typically built on the outskirts of the city, were bigger, more comfortable and much cleaner thanks largely to the often considerable staff of servants they employed. The growth of the middle class was a clear sign that for some people industrial change had brought about a real increase in their comfort and personal wealth.

Activity

Look at your completed table.
4 What does the table tell you? Did you have more positive or negative points?
5 Would moving to Manchester in 1850 really have been a change for the better?
6 Does your study of Manchester lead you to believe that 'Change is always for the better'? Give reasons for your answer.

9

Slums, smog and sewers? What was the big story of change, 1745–1901?

Change down the mine – how far had John Hall's life as a typical miner in 1880 been made safer by the Mines Acts?

John Hall was a typical miner of the nineteenth century and as such he was working every day in very dangerous conditions. However, between 1842 and 1862 the government passed a series of Mines Acts. These acts of Parliament were meant to make the working lives of miners, like John, much safer.

Think

What clues are there in picture A that John and his workmates were miners?

In this chapter you are going to investigate whether the Mines Acts did what they were intended to do. Did they make John Hall's working life as a typical miner safer? By working through this chapter you will add another piece to the jigsaw puzzle of how we should best describe the changes in the lives of ordinary people. You will also be able to evaluate the extent to which the laws the government passed had a positive impact on ordinary people's lives.

Why were coal mines dangerous?

As you have already discovered (see pages 112–15), in the period after 1750 the population of Britain began to rise and new industries such as iron and steel were developed. These were powered by new inventions in machinery, such as the blast furnace. All of these people needed coal to heat their homes and many of the new machines needed a reliable source of power, which coal provided. As a result coal mines became larger, deeper and in many cases, much more dangerous. The images on the next page show you some of the dangers faced by miners in the 1800s.

⬆ A photograph of John Hall. John Hall was the great-great grandfather of Neil Bates, one of the authors of this book. He is the gentleman standing in the middle of the group holding the stick. The photograph was taken in 1880 outside Murton Colliery in County Durham in the north-east of England. What clues are there in the picture that John and his 'maras' (workmates) were miners?

Activity

Before being able to investigate whether the Mines Acts made the mines safer for miners like John Hall, you need to find out what working conditions were like in the mines before the first Mines Act was passed. You can do this by answering the following questions.

1　Picture B is part of a drawing showing some of the supposed dangers of working in a coal mine. How many dangers can you find in the drawing? Make a list.

2　Read the text boxes surrounding picture B. What other dangers can you find? Add them to your list.

The dangers of working down a coal mine

Pit shaft collapse
In mines with only one entry, it this became blocked, (for instance by a rock fall) then miners could be trapped underground.

Fire damp
This was methane gas which might explode if it came into contact with a spark.

Flooding
Mines could be flooded by tunnels opening into underground lakes.

Choke damp
Coal seams could contain 'choke damp'. This was a mixture of gases that could suffocate miners.

B

Roof collapse
Poor roof support could lead to tunnel ceilings falling and crushing or trapping miners.

Physical damage
Children could be crushed by coal trucks or deformed from pulling/pushing heavily loaded coal trucks. All miners were at risk from accidents with machinery, and from physical damage caused by the job.

⬆ An engraving of Bradley Mine in Staffordshire drawn in the 1850s.

The Mines Acts

In 1842 a report into the conditions in mines led to widespread concern for the safety of the workers, particularly women and children who worked underground for eleven or twelve hours per day. This led to the government passing three Mines Acts between 1842 and 1872. These were intended to prevent women and young children from working in mines and to make the working lives of miners, like John Hall, much safer.

> **Think**
>
> What improvements to miners' lives were these laws designed to introduce?

1842 Mines & Collieries Act
Banned the following from working underground:
● women
● girls
● boys under ten years old.

1860 Coal Mines Regulation Act
● Banned boys less than twelve years of age from working underground.
● Required mine owners to fence off dangerous areas of their mines and ensure that all miners had a safety lamp.

1872 Mines Regulation Act
● Required all mines to have two exit shafts in case one became blocked.
● All pit managers had to be trained and qualified.

9

Slums, smog and sewers? What was the big story of change, 1745–1901?

What does the evidence tell us about whether safety in the mines improved?

The job of a historian is to reconstruct the past using the available evidence. Often, historians will be using this evidence to answer a particular question that they have. On pages 128–29 are a series of sources which will help you to answer your question 'Was John Hall's life as a typical miner made safer by the laws the government passed?'

Activity

As you read the sources, complete your own copy of the evidence grid below. The first one has been done for you. You should use your ideas from page 127 to help you fill in the last two columns.

Source and description	Date	What does it tell you about working conditions for miners in 1880?	Does it show miners' lives had become safer or improved? Give reasons	Is it related to a government Act? Give reasons
C Miner's safety lamp	1816	It gave miner's light and protected the flame from coming into contact with explosive gases.	Yes, as it helped to prevent explosions caused by fire damp.	No – it was introduced in 1816, 26 years before the first Act of 1842. However, the 1860 Act meant mine owners were required to provide them.

Now use the rest of the sources D–H to complete your table. Be careful that you pay attention to the dates.

C

Miner's safety lamp

The miner's safety lamp was invented in 1816. By protecting the flame with two thin wire gauzes it allowed the miners to have light without the risk of the flame contacting explosive gases. The safety lamp has saved the lives of thousands of miners over the years.

D

Black lung

Breathing in coal dust could clog miners' lungs leading to breathing problems. This photograph shows the lung tissue of a coal miner (top) and healthy lung tissue (bottom). Many miners suffer from black lung. This is a disease caused by breathing in coal dust. It causes coughing, wheezing and even today it is believed that hundreds of former miners die of black lung each year.

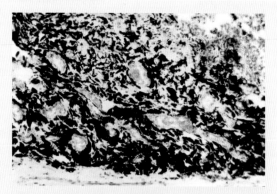

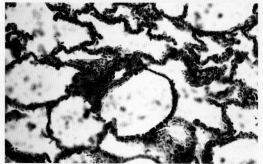

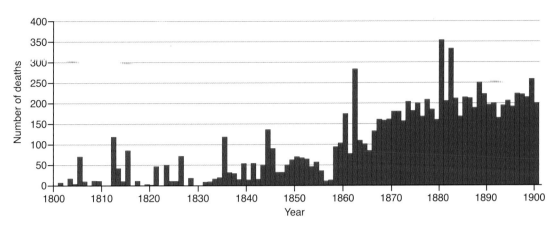

⬆ This graph shows deaths in the mines of the Durham coalfield, 1800–1900.

F

THE SEAHAM COLLIERY EXPLOSION

About 130 miners have lost their lives ... Bodies have been discovered, most of them terribly burned. A survivor said that ... one boy's head was burnt completely off. The number of horses and ponies below is estimated at more than 400, and all have been killed.

⬆ An article from *The Times* newspaper, 1880.

G

DREADFUL COLLIERY ACCIDENT

One of the worst colliery accidents which has occurred in this country took place on the morning of Thursday week (Jan 16th) at New Hartley Colliery, near Newcastle-on-Tyne, resulting in the immediate death of five poor fellows and the suffocation of 215 others. This colliery, like the majority of the mines in the northern coal district, has only one shaft [access tunnel] ...

[A beam holding up a water pump] snapped in the middle, and, pitching direct down the shaft ... pulling down after it the wooden lining of the shaft, bringing away masses of masonry. [Once the shaft was blocked, the men below ground suffocated.]

⬆ An article from the *Illustrated London News*, January 1862. (It was the Hartley disaster that led to the introduction of the 1862 Mines Act.)

Activity

Look at your evidence grid. Which of the statements below do you agree with? Copy those you agree with.

1 The Mines Acts made John Hall's life much safer.
2 Black lung and fire damp were major dangers facing miners in the 1880s.
3 The 1842 Mines Act was a step forward in making mining safer.
4 The **Personal Rescuer**, an emergency breathing apparatus, was a major help to John Hall in 1880.
5 As the country needed more coal, so more miners were likely to be killed.

Compare your list to that of someone else in the class. Did you come to the same conclusions?

Having worked through this chapter you should now be able to answer the following question:

How far did the government succeed in making mining safer between 1842 and 1880? Explain your answer.

129

9

Slums, smog and sewers? What was the big story of change, 1745–1901?

Change in the workhouse – what can the Andover Scandal teach us about changing attitudes to poverty?

How a government or a society treats its most vulnerable people can tell us a lot about the changing attitudes of people within that society.

If the big story of ordinary life was simply one of misery we can expect no real improvement in how the people of 1745–1901 tried to deal with the poor and vulnerable. In this enquiry we will try to answer the question 'Did attitudes towards the poor change for the better in this period?' We are going to start with looking at events in the Hampshire town of Andover in 1846. From there we will look both backwards to 1745 and forwards to 1901 to see if and how attitudes might have changed.

A

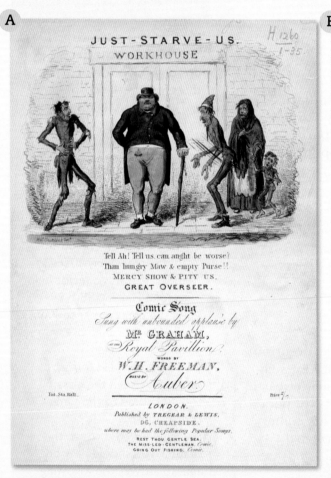

B

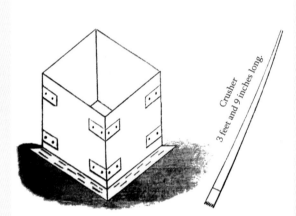

⬆ Bone crushing equipment given to inmates in the Andover Workhouse. A long iron bar or rammer weighing twenty or thirty pounds along with an iron-bound wooden box. The sides of the box could be removed to enable bone dust to be taken out. The box itself was fixed firmly to the floor of the workhouse.

◀ The cover of a song about the Andover Workhouse, published in 1973.

Enquiry Step 1: First evidence – asking questions

1 Look at pictures A and B. What connections can you suggest between the images?

2 Using these two pictures write a short statement explaining what you think happened in the Andover Workhouse in 1846?

1 Now read fact file C to find out what really did happen in the Andover Workhouse.

2 What have you learned about attitudes to poor people in 1846 from the events in Andover? Write down three ideas. Compare them with your partner's ideas. Did you have the same or different ideas?

C

Fact file: what really happened

After the passing of the 1834 Poor Law Amendment Act, help for 'able-bodied' paupers was given through workhouses. Workhouses were special buildings where the able-bodied poor were sent to live and work. Conditions in the workhouses were deliberately made harsher than the worst conditions outside. This was to try to encourage people to take any job instead of ending up there. Families were separated, work was hard and boring, uniforms had to be worn and there were punishments for misbehaving. The favoured task for the inmates to perform was the breaking up of animal bones to use as an ingredient in fertiliser for farms.

The Andover Workhouse had a reputation for being very strict, largely due to its fearsome Master Colin McDougal, a former sergeant-major who had fought at Waterloo in 1815. (You can read about the battle of Waterloo on page 105.) McDougal ran the workhouse along with his wife, Mary Ann, described by the Chairman of the Guardians as 'a violent lady'. The McDougals ran the workhouse like a prison, keeping spending and food rations to a minimum. Inmates in the workhouse had to eat their food with their fingers, and weren't even allowed the extra food and drink provided in other workhouses at Christmas or for Queen Victoria's coronation in 1838. Even speaking could earn an inmate a spell in a **punishment cell**.

In 1845 rumours began to spread in the town that inmates in the workhouse were so short of food that they had begun to eat scraps of flesh from the animal bones they were supposed to be breaking. The rumours also talked of fights breaking out when a particularly fleshy bone was found. One inmate later declared: 'To satisfy our hunger a little, because a pint and a half of gruel is not much for a man's breakfast, we eat the stale and stinking meat'. Mr Hugh Mundy, one of the **guardians** of the workhouse, was so concerned with the rumours that he raised them at a board meeting. However, he got nowhere as many of the guardians approved of McDougal's methods. Instead, Mundy involved his local MP and eventually a Parliamentary Commission of Enquiry was set up. This Commission quickly established that the rumours of under-feeding were true. In addition it heard of inmates as young as eight performing back-breaking work, as well as of the violent, drunken and lecherous antics of McDougal.

The Andover Workhouse scandal was clearly a very unpleasant example of the ways in which poor people were treated in the 1840s. As historians, however, we like to compare attitudes over time. This helps us to decide if attitudes and treatment changed or stayed the same. Andover can be seen as representing a low point in the treatment of the poor in this period, but was it the low point?

Draw a copy of the compassion graph below. This graph will allow us to examine attitudes towards the poor. Your task is to decide how compassionate or caring the government and authorities were being towards the poor at different points between 1745 and 1901.

The Andover Workhouse scandal has been placed on the graph for you, along with a few words of explanation. As you read the information boxes below and on page 133 you will need to plot the rest of the compassion graph. Remember, you are making a decision about how caring the government was towards the poor at different stages in the period 1745–1901.

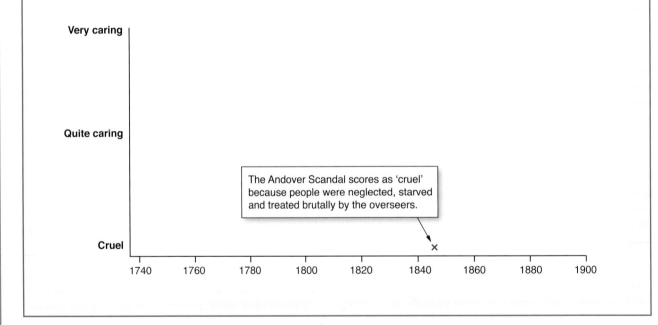

The Andover Scandal scores as 'cruel' because people were neglected, starved and treated brutally by the overseers.

1 The old poor law

In 1745 help for the poor was still based on the old Elizabethan Poor Law from 1601. Local parishes gave the sick and elderly money and food in their own homes (Outdoor Relief). In some parts of the country workhouses had been set up to provide help for the able-bodied poor (people thought to be fit enough to work). These workhouses were not common and many able-bodied poor continued to receive Outdoor Relief.

2 Gilbert's Act 1782

This act allowed parishes to work together to set up and share a central workhouse. The act displayed a humane and caring attitude to the poor, stating that the workhouse should be used to give shelter to the sick and elderly, and that the able-bodied poor should be given Outdoor Relief.

9

Slums, smog and sewers? What was the big story of change, 1745–1901?

3 The Speenhamland System 1795

In 1795 farm workers faced many problems. Bad harvests, rising population and war with France brought a sharp rise in bread prices and the threat of famine. Local authorities feared farm labourers might revolt, following the example of the French Revolution (see page 93). The solution was that the difference between a worker's wages and the amount his family needed to survive would be 'made up' by money from the parish. This 'bread scale' saved many labourers from starvation.

4 Poor Law Amendment Act 1834

Concern at the cost of the Speenhamland system and a growing belief that poor people were lazy led to the 1834 Poor Law Amendment Act. This abolished both the allowances to labourers and Outdoor Relief. Anyone wanting poor relief had to enter the workhouse with their entire family. Workhouses would be disciplined and deliberately made less comfortable than the life enjoyed by the lowest paid workers. Poor Law Commissioners were to check that the workhouse was well run and that money was wisely spent.

5 Barnardo's

By 1860 the attitude of the government was that people were poor as a result of their own laziness and that they should not look to anyone else to help them. What help there was, beyond the workhouse, came from charities and private individuals. In 1867 Dr Thomas Barnardo set up a children's home in Stepney. By 1900 Barnardo had set up over a hundred homes, giving help to 60,000 orphaned and homeless children.

6 Rowntree and Booth

In the 1880s and 1890s the work of social reformers such as Seebohm Rowntree and Charles Booth provided evidence to challenge the old idea that poverty was the fault of the poor. Old age, sickness, low wages and unemployment – not laziness and drunkenness – were the real causes of poverty. These researchers were respectable middle-class men so their ideas were listened to by politicians and influenced the Liberal government elected in 1906. This government went on to introduce old age pensions, free school meals and school medical checks to help the less well off.

Enquiry Step 4: Concluding your enquiry

It is time to sum up what you have learned from this section.

1 How would you describe your completed graph?

   What words best describe your graph? Choose from the list below or add ideas of your own.

steady	rapid	fluctuating
dramatic	slow	glacial

2 What conclusions can we draw? Did attitudes towards poverty change for the better or the worse between 1745 and 1901?

⬆ A workshop at Stepney Boys Home, London.

9

Slums, smog and sewers? What was the big story of change, 1745–1901?

How will you sum up the big story of change, 1745–1901?

History has become big business over the last few years, with television programmes such as *Who Do You Think You Are?* and *Meet the Ancestors*, as well as fictional TV series such as *The Village* and *Downton Abbey*.

One aspect of this history industry is heritage museums, places like Beamish in the north-east of England, Big Pit in south Wales and Ironbridge in Shropshire. Part of the task of these museums is to summarise the changes in the lives of ordinary people during the period of the Industrial Revolution. How should the changes you have studied be presented to people? Is the story all slums and misery as Engels portrayed it to be (see page 110) or have you discovered that there is more to the story? The activity below will give you a chance to decide.

Activity

Imagine that you have been hired by a heritage museum to produce a pamphlet for their new display which focuses on the changes that took place in the lives of ordinary British people between 1745 and 1901. To produce the pamphlet you have a number of decisions to make.

Decision 1

1 What images will you use? Look back through this chapter on the ways the Industrial Revolution changed the lives of ordinary people. Which images do you think best summarise the changes? In your notebook explain why you have chosen these images.

> Tip: Remember, as you are trying to summarise changes, you might decide to use two contrasting pictures.

Decision 2

2 What are you going to call the exhibition? The pamphlet and the exhibition need a title. Look back through the chapter headings in this section of the book. Would you use something similar or can you come up with a better title?

Write your title into your notebook and explain why you think it works.

> Tip: Remember it has to be attention grabbing and tell people that the exhibition will focus on changes in the lives of ordinary people.

Decision 3

3 You now need to write the blurb. This is the short piece of text that tells prospective visitors what to expect in the exhibition.

> Tip: Remember, this blurb needs to be short (aim for about 150–200 words) but give people a sense of the focus being on changes. What do you think was the biggest, most startling change of this period? Write the blurb into your notebook.

Once you have finished

4 Compare your choices with other people in your class. Think about the following.
- Did you choose similar or different pictures?
- Are your exhibition titles similar?
- Do your blurbs focus upon the same changes?
- Did you agree or disagree about what the biggest, most startling changes were?

Summing it all up, 1745–1901

A main aim of all the books in this series is the same – to leave you with 'a sense of period'.

Developing a 'sense of period' involves more than simply learning dates and facts – it means developing an empathy (a 'feel') for the people and their lives … understanding WHY the age was like it was.

The History National Curriculum for Key Stage 3 divides British History up into four periods. Each is distinctive, with different technologies, different political ideas, and different attitudes and beliefs. How have we done in this book for leaving you with a 'sense of period' for the period 1745–1901? Do you feel you understand what the period 1745–1901 'was about'?

Now we are going to let you develop your own interpretation of the period 1745–1901. This section will help you organise your ideas.

Activity

Working in a small group, do the following:

1 We started the book (pages 2–3) with a study of what we called the 'defining event of the period' – the Great Exhibition of 1851. The 'defining event of the period' is going to be the event which best sums up what the period was about – would you have chosen the Great Exhibition? If not, suggest some other events which, for you, better illustrate the age.

2 On page 9 we listed our suggestions of ten important 'headline' events of the period. Looking back through the book, choose what you think are the ten most important events of the era.
Justify your choices. Share your ideas with other groups, and use their ideas to refine and change your own list.

3 We divided up your studies into different aspects – Beliefs (Section 4), Power (Section 5), The United Kingdom (Section 6), Warfare and empire (Section 7) and People's lives (Section 9). Look back and review your learning in each of these sections. Each one will have helped to create your 'sense of period', but which aspects most dominate your impression of the times?

4 You also studied the French Revolution (Section 8). Mr Kennett, the author of that section, helped you assess its significance. Explain how studying the French Revolution helped your developing 'sense of period' for the years 1745–1901.

5 You learned on page 4 that there is no accepted 'name' for the period 1745–1901. Having studied this period, what would you call the years 1745–1901: the 'Age of __'?

⬆ The Crystal Palace was built to hold the Great Exhibition in 1851.

Summing it all up, 1745–1901

The entries in the tables on these pages are just our suggestions, of course! You will have your own opinions about the Middle Ages and the Early Modern Era, and you will be forming your opinion of the Modern Age in the final book of this series.

	Middle Ages, 1066–1509	Early Modern Era, 1509–1745
A	Norman Conquest, Magna Carta, Black Death	Reformation, Glorious Revolution, Union with Scotland
B	William I, Edward I, Edward III	Henry VIII, Oliver Cromwell, William of Orange
C	Peasants' Revolt	The Armada
D	Murder of Thomas Becket	Execution of Charles I
E	Royal rulers, rebellions and the beginning of Parliament	King or Parliament?
F	A time of disease and warfare	A time of religion and politics

Activity

I   Debate and take a class vote to choose the key aspects of the period:
A   the three most important events of the period
B   the three most important people of the period
C   the most interesting topic
D   the 'defining event'
E   the most important issue(s) in government.
F   Finally, choose two or three words which, for you, together sum up the period 1745–1901; make them into a sentence which starts with the words: 'A time of …' and which 'sums up the age'. Share your sentence with other groups, and use their comments and ideas to refine your own sentence.

The years 1745–1901	Modern Age, 1901–present
Activity 1a	1930s Depression, Holocaust, Welfare State
Activity 1b	Hitler, Stalin, Churchill
Activity 1c	Life behind the Iron Curtain
Activity 1d	First World War
Activity 1e	Fascism and communism
Activity 1f	A time of mass-consumption, overshadowed by the threat of nuclear warfare

Activity

2 Finally, write 250 words on

Britain in the Age of <insert the name you chose on page 135>, 1745–1901.

Start with the heading: How do we define the years 1745–1901? Then write sentences on:

▌ The three most important events, the three most important people, and the most interesting topic of the period.

▌ The defining event of the period, and how it 'sums up the age'.

▌ The most important issue(s) in government.

▌ Finish with your summative sentence from question 1f.

Glossary

Absolute monarchy A king who rules without any form of democratic government

Anglicised This is where a foreign word is written using English letters, so that it can be read by English-speaking readers

Aristocracy The highest rank of society, usually people with some kind of title – e.g. lords, dukes, etc.

Artisans Skilled workers, usually craftsmen

Assembly line A line of factory workers along which a product passes consecutively from operation to operation until completed

Atheist Someone who rejects all religious beliefs

Bankruptcy When you run out of money to the point where you can pay no more of your debts

Barbaric Primitive and uncivilised

Blacklisted When an employer in the nineteenth century suspected workers of being troublemakers (e.g. if they were in a trade union), they would sack them but also circulate their names to other employers so nobody would employ them

Bled Eighteenth-century doctors believed that illness was caused by 'bad blood', so they would 'bleed' their patients (e.g. by opening a vein) to get rid of some of it

Bourbon Monarchy The name of the branch of the French monarchy who ruled between 1815 and 1830

British Raj The period of British government rule over India, 1858–1947

Censorship Where the government controls what can and cannot be published, a lack of freedom of speech

Cholera A fatal disease caused by bacteria in the water or food; symptoms include diarrhoea that smells of fish, sunken eyes and cold skin that turns blue-grey

Collective bargaining A process where workers negotiate and fight for their rights with their employers

Communists A group that believe that property and wealth should be shared equally

Conscription Compulsory military service

Conspicuous expenditure Buying expensive and unnecessary items, so as to show off your wealth

Constituencies In the United Kingdom, a 'constituency' is an area that elects an MP

Constitutional monarch A king who acts as Head of State but lets the government makes all the laws

Coup d'etat A term for a seizing of power

Corrupt A term primarily applied to politicians and government officials who misuse their position to steal money and influence

Cult of the Supreme Being A curious religion imposed by Robespierre during the Terror; it did not involve worshipping gods but devotion to Reason

Dictatorship Where a country is ruled by a single leader with absolute authority

Direct tax a tax on your wages directly

Discrimination Treating a person unfairly because of who they are – e.g. because of their race, religion or gender

Dissenting / dissenter A person who does not belong to the Church of England, but belongs to a non-conformist group, e.g. the Unitarians

Diversity A range of different things

Division of labour Where different parts of a manufacturing process are given to different people in order to improve efficiency

Domestic system A system of (mainly) cloth production in which the spinning and weaving was done in the home as opposed to in a factory

East India Company A company set up in 1600 to trade with India and the Far East. It became very powerful and ended up controlling large parts of India using its own army

Emigrants People who choose or are forced to leave their country and travel abroad

Estates General An assembly (or meeting) or the three main estates of France – the clergy (First Estate), the nobles (Second Estate) and the common people (Third Estate) – summoned by the King to offer advice at times of crisis

Factories Workshops where raw materials are turned into products to be sold or (*slave trade*) forts in Africa where slaves were held before being transported to the Americas

Fallow fields Fields that are deliberately left empty in order for the soil to recover its nutrients

Fenians A term for members of the Fenian Brotherhood; sometimes used as a term of abuse for pro-Republican Irish Catholics

Formative Having a great effect on the future

Galleons Large sailing ships used to transport cargo

General Maximum A law imposed by the French government during the Terror to set the price limit for goods; this stopped prices rising uncontrollably

Genocide The murder of large numbers of people from a particular race or nation

Gentry Well-to-do people, such as knights and lords-of-the-manor, often living in the country

Gleaning The practice of collecting things such as firewood or blackberries from Common Land

Guardian The person in charge of running a workhouse

Indirect taxes Tax on the goods you buy, e.g. salt; this negatively affects the poor especially

Industrialists A person involved in the ownership and management of industry

Infant mortality rate Number of infant deaths for every 1000 live births

Innovations A new product or idea

Knew their station In Victorian times, poor people were expected to be deferent and humble, and to accept their disadvantaged position in society

Laissez-faire A French term meaning leave alone: it means the policy of a government leaving an economy alone, rather than interfering with lots of policies

Liberal A person who believes in the ideas of liberty (freedom)

Liberty The state of being free

Lithography A way of copying a picture, using oil and water

Lower classes A term for the poorer people in society

Methodist A Christian religious group who stress the importance of moral and social responsibility

Middle classes A term for the people in society who are neither the richest, nor the poorest, in society; in the nineteenth century, the 'middle classes' were generally a lot richer (e.g. bankers, doctors, wealthy businessmen) than we think of 'middle class' people as being today

Missionary A person who seeks to spread their religious beliefs to others

Mutual aid organisation An association (e.g. 'Friendly Societies') whose members club together, paying in when times are good, and helping out members who fall on hard times

Night Watch Men who tried to uphold the law in eighteenth-century towns, before Robert Peel introduced the police force

Non-conformist Protestant Christians who were not part of the Church of England

Orleans Monarchy The name of the branch of the French monarchy who ruled between 1830 and 1848

Parlour maid A maid who tidied the downstairs rooms visited by guests, and perhaps served tea when they visited

Persecution The mistreatment of a group of people because of race, politics or religion

Personal Rescuer Miners' emergency breathing apparatus carried on his belt next to his cap lamp battery

Physician A person qualified to practice medicine

Picketing Striking workers demonstrating outside a place of work

Poor Law guardians The people given the responsibility of running a workhouse

Porters Workers who carried bags and other loads, e.g. in a railway station or hotel, or in the docks

Punishment cell A prison cell where you are put in isolation as punishment

Quarter A weight of grain equal to 12.7 kilograms

Radical Someone who has extreme political views and often wants total reform of the current system

Radical nationalists People prepared to use extreme measures in order to gain Irish independence

Repressive A harsh government that restricts the freedom of its citizens

Republic A country which has no monarch and is ruled by the government

Resurrection The belief that Jesus Christ returned from the dead after being crucified

Rout To be decisively beaten

Royal Society The name of the organisation of the top scientists in Britain

Royalist Someone who supports the monarchy

Sans-culottes Literally meaning without trousers, this term is used to describe the French urban working class

Sepoys Indian soldiers who fought for the East India Company

Seven Years War A world-wide war, 1754–1763, in which Britain defeated her enemies (primarily France) and established an empire

Sinn Fein An Irish political party that aimed at complete Irish independence from Britain

Theologians People who study the nature of God

Threshing corn Work carried out in autumn and winter by farm labourers to separate corn from the stalks

Trade union An organisation set up to protect workers' rights

Transportation A punishment whereby prisoners were sent to Australia to do hard labour

Unitarian Church

Universal suffrage Where everyone has the right to vote no matter what class or gender you are

Index